Black Bear

COUNTRY

Black Bear
C O U N T R Y

MICHAEL FURTMAN

NORTHWORD PRESS
Minnetonka, Minnesota

Photography © 1998: Tom & Pat Leeson: front cover, 16B, 17B, 70, 111, 123; Bill Lea: front flap, 6, 22, 24, 25, 32, 40-41, 42, 43, 44A, 44B, 45, 50, 64-5, 69, 73, 78, 82, 83, 86, 87, 94, 95, 96, 102-103, 104, 105, 106-107, 112, 113, 114-115, 118-119, 121, 124-125, 128-129, 130, 132-133, 137, 157; Erwin & Peggy Bauer: 2, 34, 84-85, 88, 140; Russ Gutshall / Dembinsky Photo Associates: 12; Lisa and Mike Husar / Team Husar: 13, 30-31, 33A, 33B; Michael H. Francis: 14-15, 19, 20-21, 39, 52-53, 61, 72, 100-101, 120, 153; Art Wolfe: 16A, 48-49, 90-91, 136; Donald M. Jones: 17A, 56, 57, 68, 154-155; Bill Kinney: 37, 76-77; Robert McCaw: 26-27, 46, 74-75, 98, 99, 108-109, 116, 126, 148-149; Mark Raycroft: 28, 38, 110; Dan Dempster / Dembinsky Photo Associates: 51; Bill Marchel: 54, 146; Len Rue, Jr.: 58-59, 141; Sharon Cummings / Dembinsky Photo Associates: 80-81; Wendy Shattil / Bob Rozinski: 92-93; Jim Roetzel / Dembinsky Photo Associates: 131, 142; Tom Walker: 134, 145; Rich Kirchner / The Green Agency: 147; Wayne Lynch: back cover, 62, 29, 63, 66-67, 138-139, 150, 151.

Book design by Russell S. Kuepper

NorthWord Press
5900 Green Oak Drive
Minnetonka, MN 55343
1-800-328-3895

Library of Congress Cataloging-in-Publication Data
Furtman, Michael.
    Black bear country / by Michael Furtman.
       p.   cm.
    Includes index.
    ISBN 1-55971-667-3 (hardcover). -- ISBN 1-55971-670-3 (softcover)
    1. Black bear. 2. Black bear--Minnesota.   I. Title.
QL737.C27F87 1998
599.78'5--dc21   98-3430

Printed in U.S.A.

Dedication

To Alden Lind, who holds a special place in his heart for bears.

Contents

Introduction

THERE HAVE BEEN black bears in my life.

I remember seeing them when I was a child, both terrified and enamored, as they prowled through our northern Minnesota neighborhood tipping over garbage cans and getting treed by dogs. I would cautiously follow behind them as they moved, apparently unconcerned, through the alley and into a pocket of woods, one eye back on the children following them. Even today it isn't unusual for city kids here in Duluth, bundled up against a chilly autumn morning and standing at a school bus stop, to see a black bear with her cubs sitting on the thick branches of some sturdy maple. In fact, we expect it.

And it isn't at all unusual to have a black bear clean your apple tree of its fruit, or eat your corn, or take down all your bird feeders so that it might eat the seed. Once in a while, you'll even hear of a black bear that entered someone's house. Sometimes they enter through an open door. Quite often they'll just open it themselves, especially screen doors, with a quick swipe of a massive paw. A few years ago, in the middle of the night, I had one on my deck, standing on its hind legs, reaching up to grab a bird feeder that hung above the window. My dog had awakened me, and when I snapped on the front room lights, I could see the picture window bowing inward with the weight of the bear's front paws against it. If that window had broken, we'd have had a surprised bear in the house, and a situation so startling I hesitate to think about it. Even with the lights on, the bear went about trying to get the feeder and wouldn't leave until I sent the dog out.

Some years ago, my wife, Mary Jo, and I were stationed for the U.S. Forest Service in the Boundary Waters Canoe Area Wilderness of northern Minnesota. We lived part of the summer in an old log cabin built in the 1930s by the Civilian Conservation Corp. It was a delightful place, near the tumbling Lower Basswood Falls at the spot where the Basswood River plunged into 26-mile-long Crooked Lake.

That old cabin showed plenty of signs of past bear visits—the screen door to the kitchen had been repeatedly ripped and repeatedly sewn. And the wooden door at the front of the building showed claw marks where a bear entry had been foiled.

Weekly—and toward the end of the summer, almost daily—one or another of the bears that lived near us visited the camp. Gypsy, our Labrador retriever, didn't take kindly to the bears, nor did they much like her. Which was fine with me, since it took us two days by trail and canoe to haul our groceries to the base, and I wasn't at all thrilled with the idea of sharing them with the bears. They could find their own food, thank you very much, and the dog proved adept at keeping them away.

So while they left our cabin alone, steering clear of the dog, they still frequently crossed the ridge in front of the cabin, just a few dozen yards away. We saw them often. And we grew accustomed to the bears, enjoying their visits, which is probably more than could be said by some of the other people who came to the Boundary Waters.

This wilderness is a popular one, and Lower Basswood Falls is one of its most frequently sought areas. So it should come as no surprise that city slickers on canoe trips bumped nose-to-nose with a curious bear from time to time. Most often, these encounters resulted in a bit of excitement for all involved, with the bears being pelted by rocks or yelled at, but with little harm being done to bear or foodstuffs. Sometimes, though, a clever bear would sneak into camp and make off with a food pack before anyone was the wiser. Often, the campers had even hung their food in a tree, which, done

properly, would defeat most bears. But not all.

There was one bear that seemed to have learned the skill of jumping out of the tree onto a suspended pack. Climbing to a branch above the pack, he or she would free-fall down to it, giving it a bearhug as it passed by. Under such circumstances, "something had to give," and most often it was the rope or the pack straps to which the rope was tied. This bear no doubt dined on freeze-dried lasagna and chocolate bars far more often than your average bear.

Then there was the bear that stole the wrong pack. Two worried male campers flagged us down and reported an early-morning bear raid. They were baffled because the bear grabbed a pack that contained their fishing equipment, camera gear, wallets and car keys. Upon questioning them, we were able to pin down the fact that they had forgotten to move some of the previous day's luncheon items from that pack back to the food pack, and also that their cooking pots (how carefully had they washed them?) were stored within it. Frightened by the encounter, they suggested we go find that bear and retrieve the gear. "After all," one of them said, "it is *your* bear."

We gently suggested that unless they wanted to buy new cameras or hire a locksmith to get them into their car, they'd better start searching the forest behind the campsite, since we felt fairly confident the bear had little use for any of their equipment and had left it behind as soon as it had finished the granola and licked the pots clean.

But perhaps the story I recall best was of the lady who had a problem with bears existing at all. I approached her at a campsite, one that was within a short hike of our cabin. I frequently hiked to this camp to check on folks and to warn them about a particularly determined bear that had been stealing food packs. I explained to this woman and her friends that the bear was harmless, that it was mostly just a nuisance, and that if they hung their food packs well (pointing out the best location to do so) there would be no problems at all. In fact, if the bear was unsuccessful in gaining their food, they'd probably never know it had been around at all, since it always came at night.

Looking at me with incredulity on her face, the woman stated with excitement, "What do you mean there are bears out here? You just let them run loose?"

I asked her what we should do with the bears.

"Why don't you live-trap them and move them someplace?" she replied.

I have to admit, I was stumped.

"Gee, lady," I said, "where do you want us to put them? I mean, we're *in* a wilderness area. These bears live here, and you're in their home."

I have to admit, I was hoping the bear made a successful raid in that camp that night.

But that was not the first summer I spent in bear country, for every year of my life has been shared with bears. I like that. Black bears are remarkable, intelligent, and exceptionally adaptable animals. I feel fortunate for having encountered them as often as I have, even when they've made a mess of my bird feeders or scared me half to death as I've bumped into them while walking out a dark trail from some secret brook trout fishing hole. Most of the time, they've been just as frightened of me as I've been of them.

Tourists and photographers weren't the first to make the acquaintance of these northwoods bears. The native Ojibwe people called the black bear "muckwa" and revered it, as well as ate it. Bears are good food, if you're so inclined. And they are remarkable for their feat of hibernation. Both of these qualities fascinated the Ojibwe and other native peoples. No doubt a good store of bear fat saved many a family during a long, cold northern winter. And the miracle of apparent death followed by a spring resurrection didn't go unnoticed by these careful observers of nature. The bear was wise. The bear was smart. It had skills far beyond those of a human. How else could they explain that bears easily survived winter, when they themselves were severely tested by it? The bear deserved respect.

On the ancient granite shorelines of the Boundary Waters and nearby Quetico Provincial Park, one can still see today the rock paintings, called pictographs, drawn in red ochre by Ojibwe shamans. Neither large nor artistic, the pictographs instead tend to be a record of a vision quest, a trip into the spiritual world.

The power of the bear's spirit was not lost on the Ojibwe. Hopefully, it will not be lost on us. Our world is changing, and the changes are wrought by you and me.

We daily expand our world into bear country, building homes where mother and cubs once napped or fed. Our backyard may now fall within an old boar's territory, and the new shopping center may encompass what was an important meadow where bears ate the spring's first green grasses.

Some of these things, sadly, may be inevitable. But many are not. As I asked the woman in the Boundary Waters, "Where do you want us to put them?" I'll ask you. Where do you want them to live? The black bear continues to thrive in many places in America, despite our intrusions, because evolution saw fit to endow it with two remarkable traits: it is shy, and it is adaptable. Given a chance, it can live near us without much conflict. And if we are tolerant, it will do so quite happily.

CHAPTER ONE

A Family of Carnivores

Hungry black bears relish the chance
to feed on fish.

WE THINK OF BEARS, in our dreams and myths and the tales we tell our children, as fierce, powerful predators lurking in dark caves. In reality, only a portion of that myth is true—bears are predators and they are powerful. But seldom do they live in caves, and over the eons, evolution has seen to it that most bears are only part-time predators. With the exception of the polar bear, the bears of the world live primarily on plants. And that is true of the black bear, too.

The American black bear entered North America via the Bering land bridge, and shares a recent common ancestor with the Asiatic black bear.

CLASSIFICATION

Although the American black bear (*Ursus americanus*) derives a great deal of its nutrition from berries, nuts, and even grasses, it is classified as a carnivore, a nod to its evolutionary roots. And to be fair, black bears are still capable of carnivorous behavior—they do stalk and kill other animals for sustenance and frequently eat animals that have died of other causes. But they don't make a full-time job of it, so to speak, in the manner of wolves or lions. Black bears are more accurately described as omnivores. Like humans, they'll eat just about anything.

Carnivores are frequently, though not always, at or near the top of the food chain. Because of that lofty position, they are fewer in number than other species. It is estimated that there are about 4,500 mammal species in the world, yet only 5 percent of them are classified as carnivores. These carnivores can be put into just a handful of family groups, and all of them evolved from a group of creatures known as the miacids, which lived about 70 million years ago. Today, there are seven families of carnivores, one of which includes the black bear.

Some of these families are very familiar to us. The family Canidae, comprising thirty-five species, includes the pet dog, the wolf, and the coyote. Some members of family Felidae, also comprising thirty-five species, reside in our homes as the pet cat, while others prowl the world as lions, tigers, lynx, and jaguars.

Less familiar to many of us is the raccoon group, family Procyonidae, which includes sixteen species other than the masked bandit for which this family is named; a group of small, fierce carnivores like the weasel, family

The American black bear shares an ancient ancestor—the miacids—
with other predators such as wolves, lions, and weasels.

The blue phase bear—known as the glacier bear—lives in heavily glaciated coastal areas.

Polar bears live farther north than any other bear, and their range is circumpolar.

Mustelidae; the Mongoose group, known as the family Viverridae; and the hyenas, the smallest group, with eight species, called family Hyaenidae.

The last family, family Ursidae, contains the subject of this book, the American black bear, as well as other familiar bears such as the polar bear and the brown bear. This family is further divided into two groups: northern and southern. Northern bears include the polar, brown (European and Asian brown bears, grizzly, and Kodiak bears are all considered one species), Asiatic black bear, and American black bear. The southern bear species are the spectacled bear, the giant panda, the sloth bear, and the sun bear. There is some disagreement among taxonomists whether or not the sloth and sun bears belong in the family Ursidae at all, but I'll leave the arguments to them.

Northern bears are, by and large, more similar to each other than they are to the southern bears. No matter where they are found in the world, northern bears share similar environments. In many cases, the ranges of northern bears overlap, as with the brown bear and the black bear, or the brown bear and the polar bear. It is unlikely that black

The grizzly of North America is considered the same species as the brown bears of Europe and Asia.

The Kermode bear—a near-white black bear—is quite rare.

bears and polar bears ever encounter each other, although in time they might. It seems as though in recent years, as the population of barren ground grizzly bears declines, some black bears have been moving out onto these arctic plains and doing quite well. There they may indeed someday stumble upon the occasional polar bear, some of whom migrate inland for short periods of time. Northern bears are also similar to each other and different from southern bears in that they hibernate and store winter fuel in the form of fat.

But all bears, northern or southern, share some features. For instance, all are plantigrades, or animals that walk on the soles of their feet (like us, as opposed to deer or dogs, which walk on their toes and are called digitigrades). A bear paw is broad and flat, and each of the five toes is armed with a curved, tough claw. This aids bears in digging, and for some species, allows them to climb trees. All also have longish, thick fur coats, many of which sport a white spot on the chest, and short, sometimes almost invisible, tails. All also have heavy, powerful limbs, and bears are considered the largest of the world's carnivores. The head of a bear is large in proportion to its body, and they have small eyes and round, upright ears. Finally, bears are long-lived species known to reach twenty-five years of age in the wild.

EVOLUTION

We humans have both a remarkably short attention span—thanks to our curiosity, an evolved adaptive trait that is largely responsible for our success as a species—and a compressed sense of time—long timelines, like those common to evolution, frequently give us a headache. Many people have difficulty imagining a timeline much longer than a few generations.

And many people have little appreciation for the long path the black bear took to arrive at its current form. Let us just say that over a million years ago, when our not-quite-human ancestors were still pounding out crude stone tools and living in troops like baboons, there were creatures already roaming the forests that were beginning to look like the bears we know today. And they'd been there for at least a million years. Humans, on the other hand, have been truly modern humans for only about 100,000 years.

So about 1.5 million years ago, during a time period known as the Pliocene, two ancestral bear forms appeared: the huge *Indarctos* line and the smaller, climbing-adapted *Protursus*. From this last line came bears that are familiar to us, *Ursus*, although their evolution was far from complete.

Looming just around the corner time-wise was the next age, the Pleistocene, that period of geologic time that we call the "ice age." The ice age had significant impact on the evolution of the modern North American black bear by the creation of the land bridge that allowed its ancestors to wander to North America to complete their evolution. This time period's cold weather also had an influence on the adaptations to body shape and behavior. The coming of cold weather was a great environmental challenge that not only had an impact on bears, but changed the course of evolution of many species, including those that became such familiar creatures as elk and deer, and humans as well. Many creatures perished in the wake of the ice age, opening niches in the environment for newer, more adaptable species, which took their place.

One of the species of bears that evolved during this period from the *Protursus* was *Ursus etruscus*—the Etruscan bear. From it derived the black, brown, and cave bears, and from this point on, speciation, that is, distinct separation into species, progressed rather rapidly, at least in geologic terms. Consider that it took as long as 60 or 70 million years for the miacids—the ancestors of all carnivores—to evolve into the seven family groups of carnivores. The fact that the bears evolved into eight distinct species since the Pliocene is indeed a geologic and evolutionary sprint.

So just what constitutes a species? Generally speaking, it is a group of animals considered genetically distinct. They are no longer capable of breeding with related species, or, at the very least, if they do mate, the offspring are not fertile, such as when the mating of a horse and burro produces a mule.

OVERLEAF: Primarily a forest dweller, the American black bear is quite shy.

Black bears use their keen senses to warn them of trouble such as grizzlies, humans, or wolves.

Long timelines and geographic separation also contribute to speciation. Little traits that may allow an animal to adapt well to a specific location are chosen by natural selection and magnified as "like breeds to like." Another population, separated by distance, may adapt differently. Gradually they develop different traits and become dissimilar (becoming subspecies), but at this point may still be able to produce fertile offspring if crossed.

For example, the brown bears of Kodiak Island are much larger than (and were once thought to be a distinct species from) their relatives, the grizzly bears of the Rocky Mountains. A cross between them, however, would produce viable offspring, since they are still of the same species. That's also true of the subspecies of black bear that can reproduce with each other. However, if the separation is long enough and the adaptations significant, subspecies eventually become so dissimilar that they become two different species. The common ancestor that two species shared at some point dies out— it gives way to the new species, which by their very success are better adapted.

For the bears of the world, this speciation has largely occurred in the last 4 to 6 million years. For the black bear, the last "jumping-off point" may have been as recent as about 3 million years ago, when it and the Asiatic black bear shared a common ancestor, *Ursus abstrusus*, which lived on both the North American and Asian continents. Even today, the Asiatic, or Himalayan, black bear (*Ursus thibetanus*) is the American black bear's nearest relative, and, although their ranges are separated by the gulf of an ocean, both species fill very similar ecological niches in their respective homes.

ARRIVAL IN NORTH AMERICA

When European settlers first set foot on the North American continent, they encountered two bears in its vast forests: One was a familiar bear, the grizzly, which is considered the same species as the brown bear of Europe. And one was unfamiliar, the black bear, which has no counterpart across the Atlantic. Of course this was not the first human contact with the black bear, since it was very familiar already to North American Indians, who not only utilized it as a much-valued food source, but who also revered it as a wise, kindred spirit. Native American lore is full of tales about the black bear and in many tribes, the black bear was a clan totem. Its fur was valued as warm clothing or robes, and its fat was at times a critical source of food for many more northerly tribes.

The America black bear, *Ursus americanus*, is a rather shy bear of the deep forest and is unique to North America. It shares with the Asiatic black bear the common ancestor, *Ursus abstrusus*, which at some point must have wandered to North America during one of the earliest ice ages. During these glacial periods, vast amounts of the earth's water was locked up in ice, lowering the oceans by nearly 300 feet, exposing new land.

Frequently during these episodes, a land bridge between Alaska and Siberia formed. Don't think of this as a dank, mucky narrows across which animals had to flee before the water swallowed them up. Instead, this land mass, known as Beringia, was exposed for

The black bear adapted well to its forested habitat.

such long periods of time that it became a vital terrestrial ecosystem, with lush plains and even forested regions. Through it, species gradually, in the process of just eating, living, and reproducing, extended their range to North America. And that's exactly how the ancestor of the black bear arrived, probably during one of the very earliest ice ages.

Skeletal evidence found in Pennsylvania

For both young and old black bears, the ability to climb trees is a survival tool to avoid danger.

caves indicates that this progenitor bear had reached that far eastern location some 500,000 years ago. To give you a better sense of the black bear's timing, it would be another 400,000 years before the brown bear arrived in North America, coinciding with the arrival of elk, bison, and moose. Humans didn't arrive until some 50,000 years ago, but they, too, crossed the Bering bridge, probably following the animals that provided them with food.

The black bear's propensity for forests may lie in the fact that when its ancestors arrived in North America, it wasn't the only bear to be found on the continent. Indeed, a fierce, leggy predator bear had already laid claim to much of this continent, as well as to the parts of the Old World—the short-faced bear, now extinct.

If the black bear was to make a go of it, it would need to confine itself to habitat unoccupied by the short-faced bear, which preferred the open. That habitat is the one black bear still occupies today—the forest. And the black bear's less aggressive behavior, one that dictates that it flee rather than fight except under extreme duress, could also be a development of that competition. It simply was no match for the short-faced bear. And any black bear ancestor that thought it was a match would have been quickly eliminated, ending up as nothing more than a meal and scattered tufts of fur. So fierce was the short-faced bear that it is speculated the grizzly's ancestor—a bear itself known for ferocity—didn't migrate down from Alaska into what is now the lower forty-eight states until after the short-faced bear's extinction.

The black bear's shyness and propensity to escape up trees served it well again against yet another competitor. For when the grizzly bear arrived across the Bering land bridge, the black bear was already here. Grizzlies adapted to open areas and became aggressive in behavior since trees in such surroundings were scarce, and therefore it must fight rather than flee. If the black bear had any hopes at all of moving out onto the open plains and hillsides, they were dashed by the grizzly's arrival. As with the short-faced bear, the black bear's escape mechanism and tendency to stay in the deeper forest served it well when sharing a region with the grizzly.

SHAPE

Like other bears, the black bear has a fairly large head crowned with round ears— the black bear's ears being larger than those of some other bear species. These upright ears serve as scoops to trap sound waves, but the roundness belies the fact that this bear evolved in a cool to cold climate, since long ears are more susceptible to freezing.

The black bear's head is rather tapered, almost triangular when seen from the side. This is most noticeable when comparing it to the grizzly bear, which has a rounder, dish-shaped face with a more pronounced fore-head. The black bear's muzzle, like that of the polar bear, runs almost straight off its forehead with very little dip. Cubs, however, like the offspring of many other mammals, are born with a foreshortened muzzle. Set on either side of the black bear's muzzle, which is frequently a lighter color than the main body fur,

are small, reddish chestnut-hued eyes.

The black bear has both a mobile tongue and dexterous lips, which aid in stripping berries and leaves from limbs and lapping up swarming insects, which can be an important part of their diet. Because black bears feed extensively on vegetation, their teeth have undergone some evolutionary changes away from those of a full-time predator.

The black bear's ears are large compared to those of some other bear species.

OVERLEAF: Although muscular and powerful, the black bear lacks the pronounced "hump" over its front shoulders typical of the grizzly bear.

Carnassial premolars and molars have been replaced by bunodont molars more suited for crushing and grinding, although the black bear still retains the large, impressive canine teeth needed to grasp and tear flesh. The gap between the canine and molars—called the diastema—is frequently used to strip vegetation from branches.

Cubs are born toothless, but by 6 to 8 weeks, their first "milk" teeth have erupted, which are replaced by their 42 permanent teeth during their second winter.

Except when lush with fat going into a winter of hibernation, a black bear's entire torso is wedge-shaped when seen in profile: tallest and widest at the hips, tapering toward the head. Both the brown bear and the polar bear exhibit a pronounced hump over the front shoulders, a feature lacking in the black bear.

The black bear's paws and claws also differ from those of the other North American bears. The polar bear's paws are much larger than the black bear's, since this nearly aquatic bear uses them as paddles or flippers. The brown bear's paws have much longer, and much more curved, claws than those found on the black bear. That's because the brown bear evolved for a more open-country setting, where it frequently digs up tubers and rodents, while the black bear lives in the forest and uses its claws to climb. For instance, the largest of brown bears—often called Kodiak bears—live on the Pacific coast of Canada and Alaska. They have long, pale-colored claws that can be as long as 5 inches. By comparison, the black bear's claws are sharper but much shorter, rarely over 2 inches in length.

The front claws of a black bear are longer than those on the back paws, and show more frequently in its tracks. Somewhat catlike in design (though not retractable), the short, sharp claws of the black bear grip best on trees with rough, tough bark. Black bears can climb trees even if there are no ladderlike limbs, something

Short claws make good tree-climbing tools,
as these juveniles demonstrate.

the grizzly can't do, and climbing is a skill frequently used to escape danger or to reach some tasty out-of-the way ripening nut or sprouting bud.

Cubs are born with claws. And by the time researchers first examine cubs—usually at 6 to 8 weeks—the claws are well developed. They have already been useful, no doubt, in pulling the cub to its mother's teats for nourishment.

All bears, not just the black bear, have five toes and a wide, flat paw. Each winter, during the last stages of hibernation, the black bear sheds the calluses from its foot pads. The new pads are quite sensitive and the bear may spend considerable time licking them. They may even bleed when the emerging bear first walks on them.

For being such a large animal, the black bear is remarkably quiet when walking, thanks to these broad, soft pads. This shape also makes it much easier for them to stand on their hind legs, which they do frequently to reach food or to get a better look at (or better sniff of) something. Standing upright is also a defense mechanism, since it makes a bear look much larger than when on all fours. This intimidates not only humans, but other potential predators, and even others of their own species when competing for food or mates, or when they must defend their home territory or cubs from another bear.

On average, a black bear's front paw tracks measure about 4 inches by 4 inches. The back paws, being larger, leave a track about 5 to 7 inches long by about 4 inches wide. The heel pad of the back foot is larger than that on the front, a good clue for

deciphering front from back when examining tracks. In addition, the black bear places most of its front foot's weight on the toes, making that foot's pad less noticeable. When walking, the back foot reaches just forward of the front.

Although their rather rotund shape and flat feet may make you think that black bears are slow and awkward, nothing could be

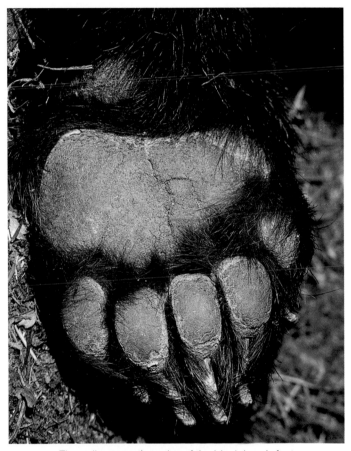

The calluses on the soles of the black bear's feet are shed during hibernation.

further from the truth. Well muscled, they easily and gracefully handle their mass and girth, and they are extremely fast sprinters, a feature used when escaping danger or running down the infrequent prey. Black bears have been clocked at 30 miles per hour, which is faster than the quickest human and equal to horses.

All of these muscles are covered in thick fur, which is composed of both a thick, woolly undercoat in winter and long, shiny guard hairs. The undercoat provides exceptional insulation, and although black bears seek good shelter for hibernation, they have been known to simply curl up in a ball on a pile of leaves and snooze the winter away. Their insulative coat is a great aid in this, although it is the slowing of their metabolism that makes hibernation possible.

Bears shed their fur in spring to rid themselves of the undercoat in preparation for warm summer, and in fall they regrow the dense undercoat. Both steps probably take place due to the influence of photoperiod—the ratio of hours of light to length of day—which in most mammals triggers changes in hormone production.

Guard hairs are relatively tough and slick. They provide good protection from brush, a fair amount of water repellency, and are sort of self-cleaning. Burrs and mud slide through them to eventually fall off, which is why, even when you see a black bear rooting around in the dirt, the guard hairs appear sleek and glossy.

Color

Black bears are black. And they are brown. They even come in blue, honey, cinnamon, blond, and white. In fact, the only thing for

Although most are black, the American black bear can be brown, white, blue, and blond.

The amount of the pigment melatonin determines how dark
a black bear's coat will be, and can be uneven throughout the coat.

sure about black bear coloration is that a sow can give birth to just about any of the above colors. She can even give birth to mixed-color litters, but black clearly is predominant. The amount of melatonin, a pigment, dictates how dark the coat is. Genetics plays a big role in determining a black bear's color, although it has been discovered that some brown-colored black bears turn all black as they age, so perhaps color is not always dictated solely by genetics.

Researchers have noted that eastern, Canadian, and Alaskan black bears are almost always black, while those in the American West are more frequently brown or tan. For instance, 95 percent of Arizona's black bears are some shade of brown, while in Minnesota, only 6 percent are a color other than black. Moving north up the Rocky Mountains from Arizona, 28 percent of Utah's black bears are black, while the rest are some lighter shade. Some speculate that this is a genetic adaptation to the warmer climate in the West—light colors reflect heat, which is an advantage in warm areas, while dark colors absorb heat, which is an advantage where it is cold. Others speculate that perhaps a more grizzlylike coloration gives a black bear

One year, the coat of this bear was quite light.

The following year, the coat darkened considerably.

an advantage in grizzly country.

There are a couple of outstanding color exceptions in small, geographically isolated populations of black bears. Once thought to be a distinct species, but now known to be a subspecies of black bear, is the Kermode bear, a beautiful near-white black bear. The Kermode bear is not an albino, which would have a pink nose and eyes, but instead has a dark nose and normal eyes. These bears are found only in an isolated section of west-central coastal British Columbia, and offshore on nearby islands. The evolutionary factors that led to this rare coloration still are not understood. Known as the "ghost" or "snow" bear, the Kermode was thought to be spiritually powerful by the aboriginal people of this region.

Even rarer than a white black bear is the blue-phase known as the glacier bear. This animal also is found in British Columbia, but farther north than the Kermode bear, where it also ranges into adjoining sections of Alaska. Living along a heavily glaciated coastal area, the glacier bear's color is sort of a gunmetal blue-gray. Even here, however, the blue-phase is not predominant; the vast majority of bears are indeed black.

SIZE

Although the black bear is the smallest of North America's bears, it still can grow to near gigantic proportions when given the right nutrition. In fact, a black bear changes immensely over the course of the year, from being gaunt upon emerging from hibernation in the spring, to absolutely roly-poly in the fall if food has been abundant. For the black bear, binge eating is a way of life. And although on average it would be accurate to state that the black bear is smaller than the grizzly bear, there are black bears that exceed some grizzlies in size.

It is the wide variance in weight during the course of a year that makes it hard to pin down an average weight for the black bear. Quite obviously, one bear can be quite a bit larger in the autumn than in the spring. Most weights recorded through hunting reveal autumn weights, the traditional season for bear hunts (although in a few areas, spring hunting is allowed). Most weights recorded by biologists reflect a midwinter weight, since frequently these bears are sedated and examined while in their dens.

Nonetheless, a few generalizations can be made. Males are almost always larger than females (on average, 50 to 70 percent heavier), and eastern black bears are generally a bit larger than western bears. This latter fact may reflect the abundance of foods in the East that are unavailable to western black bears, such as great quantities of mast (nuts) like acorns, beechnuts, and hazelnuts, as well as lush forbs growing in the forest understory that wouldn't be found in drier climates.

Depending on whose research you read, adult male black bears range in size from 130 to 300 pounds, 150 to 550 pounds, or 250 to 450 pounds. Let's just say that male black bear weight is highly variable. The same discrepancies hold for female black bear weight. However, these ranges don't belie the true magnitude attainable by the black bear, especially males. It has been noted by researchers that the testicles of males can be retracted for protection. Thus, some anecdotal reports of unusually large females are likely based on sightings of males whose testicles are simply hidden from view.

There are, however, accurate accounts of black bears weighing up to 800 pounds, which is considerably larger than some grizzly bears. Although these are rare individuals, it isn't all that uncommon for black bears, in the prime of their autumn glut, to top the scales at nearly 500 pounds. Watching a bear this "well-rounded" is a pleasure. With a thick, prime winter coat, and layers upon layers of fat, they roll along like grandma's overfed pooch, luxurious in their excess. They will not look nearly as handsome come spring.

From the tip of the nose to the end of the tail, black bears measure about 5 or 6 feet, and stand about 2 or 3 feet tall. I've heard folks describe 150-pound black bears as small, and that's true in a relative sense, but when they do so after a chance encounter in the woods, calling such a bear "small" is generally an attempt to minimize the human's fear. After all, folks are rightly afraid of a 75-pound guard dog, and this "small" black bear outweighs it by 100 percent.

Although the smallest of North American bears, the black bear can still achieve a weight of 800 pounds.

Vocalization

Black bears are normally quiet, with none of the dramatic calls of some other large animals, like wolves or elk. They do, however, communicate with each other through a combination of subtle sounds, such as the mewing of cubs as they nurse or the grunting of a sow as she reprimands a youngster. They can also emit loud growls or "huffs" when startled, threatened, or when trying to warn off an interloping bear or human. Black bears also click their teeth during such encounters. Cubs bawl loudly whenever frightened, and this is one of the few sounds black bears make that carries some distance, an obvious advantage in drawing the attention of a mother bear that might be feeding out of sight of her cubs.

Memory and Intelligence

Quantifying intelligence is hardly an exact science. But anyone who has spent much time either studying bears or trying to thwart them from raiding an apple tree, bird feeder, or garbage can, will attest to the fact that these animals seem to be pretty smart, probably as smart at the family dog.

Faced with complicated tasks such as opening supposedly "bear-proof" garbage cans, removing food from cars parked near a woodland trailhead, or getting a food pack down out of a tree, black bears display both creativity and persistence.

It is apparent that they are capable of learned behavior, such as avoiding objects or places once they've had an unpleasant encounter, or repeating a task that has led to success. Cubs routinely learn the routes around their mother's home range and the location of food and other resources. They learn simply by following her, as she probably learned these routes and places from her mother.

Black bears also have been known to travel tens of miles to unique food sources that are repeated only once a year—such as a spawning run of fish or a rare grove of nut- or fruit-producing trees. While the bear may have merely chanced upon this food source the first time, the fact that he or she then returns to it indicates a good memory and the ability to relocate a place in what you or I would consider a trackless forest.

Rather than an innate sense of direction, such repeat journeys probably are possible because of memory—each step along the way triggering a memory of what the next turn should be.

Disposition

Normally, the black bear is an undemonstrative animal. But cubs—even yearlings—seem to enjoy play. For the most part, the black bear is primarily concerned with its own safety and finding its next meal.

An adult black bear, however, is capable of aggression. For most of the year, males quietly mind their own business, staying away from other bears of both sexes. There are exceptions, of course. Male bears have been known to attack the cubs of female bears, and boars may fight each other when competing for a female in estrus. But these events are quite rare.

Similarly, female black bears can display aggression toward other bears or even

Cubs learn of new foods
and travel routes from their mothers.

The black bear's keen sense of hearing is aided by scoop-shaped ears
that can be slightly rotated to help locate sounds.

humans when defending their cubs. They are, however, much more likely to attack another bear than a human for such a transgression.

It is true that black bears have attacked people and have even killed and consumed them. But to characterize this as anything but an extremely rare occurrence would do the shy black bear an injustice. Millions of humans live in the range of the black bear, and yet black bear attacks are so rare that when they occur, even bear experts are surprised.

For most of the year, black bears— other than a sow with cubs—wander alone, in search of food. Bear families also wander alone in their own company. In all but the rarest of instances—such as when a food source is concentrated—bears pretty much avoid each other. They also avoid humans. When encountering people, black bears almost invariably flee quickly and quietly.

Senses

When you encounter a bear in the woods, it is there because it chose to be there, for there can be little doubt that it

An exquisite sense of smell allows black bears to detect foods miles away.

already knew you were coming. Black bears have remarkably keen senses.

Topping the list is probably its sense of smell, a sense tuned to perfection not only for detecting enemies for the purpose of survival, but also to find food, which for the bear can be at times difficult to locate. There are numerous accounts of black bears able to detect a food, such as a berry crop, not only from hundreds of yards away, but of miles, given the right winds and climatological conditions. Scents carry best on damp days when scent molecules bond with water molecules. Dampness also increases the efficiency of olfactory nerves.

Scenting ability also plays a role in reproduction, since the male bear detects the readiness and availability of females through chemical clues, either airborne or revealed in the sow's urine. To accomplish these feats, the black bear has a long snout stuffed with sensitive nerves, some one hundred times greater in surface area than in the human nose.

But if the nose reigns supreme, the black bear's sense of hearing surely is the next most keen. Each ear is a collector, and although the bear's ears aren't as mobile as those of a

OVERLEAF: Male black bears often sniff the breeze for detecting food as well as possible mates.

white-tailed deer, they can be swiveled slightly to help detect the location of a sound. Ears also play a telltale role in behavior display. For instance, aggression is often revealed by ears laid flat, while concern (or at least curiosity) is displayed when the ears stand at attention with a slight forward tilt. It is thought that black bears, like dogs, can hear high-pitched sounds. In any case, a black

Although thought to be its weakest sense, the eyesight of black bears seems to provide them with very good peripheral vision.

bear's sense of hearing is much superior to that of humans.

It has long been said that a bear's eyesight is its weakest sense. That may well be true. But more recent evidence seems to indicate that a bear's eyesight is better than once believed. Bears, like most predators, are much better at detecting a moving object than one that is stationary. Based on field observations, bear researchers tend to agree that bears also seem to have very good peripheral vision. That is, they can see well to the side even while the eyes face forward.

This makes good sense, because bears spend a lot of time foraging. Most grazing or browsing animals have an eye on each side of the head that operates somewhat independently of the other and provides an enormous range of view. But the eyes of bears, like those of humans or dogs, face forward, separated only by the breadth of the muzzle. Good peripheral vision would help offset the narrow range of view, allowing them to concentrate on the near objects while they eat, yet still providing an "eye out" for trouble.

Bears likely have binocular vision similar to that of humans. Binocular vision provides good depth of field and distance judgment, something a bear would find very useful for picking berries or eating grubs at short range, just as it is for us when we read or manipulate something.

Although it is thought that many mammals (other than humans) have difficulty in perceiving hues, there is evidence that black bears can see color. This, too, may have an evolutionary root. Dogs and their ancestor, the wolf, don't see color. There is no advantage to it since the color of the meal—such as a deer—doesn't change much. Color is unimportant to their food gathering. But berries change color as they ripen, as do many of the other foods that bears feed upon. Having color vision would help a black bear detect which foods are at their nutritional peak. There is little benefit in gorging on unripened food when a nearby ripened (and different-colored) source might be much more nutritious.

Since much of what this rather large animal eats is ironically quite small—berries, grubs, nuts—they have developed extremely dexterous lips and tongue. With these they can delicately pluck ripened fruit from the stem or strip leaves from a branch. When doing the latter, the bear often slides the branch through a gap in its teeth, neatly stripping off the leaves.

FEEDING BEHAVIOR

The black bear is virtually always hungry. Because of the constraints of reproduction and hibernation (which will be discussed later), black bears have a remarkably short period of time each year to pack away the calories needed to get them through the winter. The specifics of what they eat will depend largely on two things: season and geographic location. Obviously, a bear in Montana will find different food than will one in Pennsylvania. But no matter where they are found, all black bears consume nuts, grasses, forbs, insects, and fruits. Given a chance, they'll also eat fish and meat.

In fact, the black bear's digestive tract, though longer than that of most carnivores,

still reflects its predatory roots. Animals completely adapted to a vegetative diet have enormously long digestive tracts and, often, multichambered stomachs, in order to effectively wring the last molecule of nutrition from plant foods. Most plants are poor sources of protein, so vast quantities must be eaten and they must be thoroughly processed to yield what nutritional value

Black bears consume a variety of fruits, flowers, nuts, green vegetation, and insects.

Squaw root is a favorite black bear food.

Acorns are an important food across large parts
of black bear country.

they offer. Even then, great quantities of waste are excreted. But a wolf, for instance, needs only a short digestive tract to handle meat, which is a highly concentrated source of protein.

The black bear has made the journey only partway toward being a vegetarian. Its intestinal tract is longer than that found in most other carnivores, but considerably shorter than that of grazers and browsers. It is only a part-time predator at this point in its evolution, but recent evidence indicates it is more predatory than some would like to admit. There are some who claim that black

bears eat meat only when they stumble upon it. However, studies have shown that black bears make a consistent practice of stalking, killing, and eating newborn deer, much in the same manner that grizzlies search out and kill elk calves in the West.

Human-conditioned study bears followed by the Minnesota Department of Natural Resources biologists in Camp Ripley (a large, forested National Guard training area in north-central Minnesota) were observed carefully searching for newborn white-tailed deer during the brief period of fawn susceptibility. One of the Minnesota study bears

Food habits and locations may be passed on
from mother to cub.

stalked, killed, and consumed seven fawns in one day, a record that could hardly be termed coincidental. In their 1988 study, N. E. Matthews and W. F. Porter chronicled whitetail fawn predation in the Adirondacks.

Predation isn't limited to white-tailed deer, however. A study of radio-collared mule deer fawns in Utah by M. L. Wilton noted that 9.3 percent of the study fawns were killed by black bears. And in Alaska, several studies have shown that black bears are a significant predator of moose calves, while in Idaho it has been determined that black bears have killed elk calves.

RANGE

At one time, black bears were found in just about every forested area of North America. Their range seemed limited only by the end of the tree line as it approached the Arctic Circle, and by the summer heat in Mexico, where they are still found in dwindling numbers in cooler mountain forests.

Even today, the black bear is far more numerous than any other North American bear, numbering about 550,000. In fact, it may well be the most plentiful bear species left in the world, thanks largely to scientific wildlife management as applied on this continent, and the fact that great amounts of forest cover still exist in Canada. Black bears live in 40 of the 49 states that they once called home, although only about 25 of those states have viable populations.

In Canada, the black bear can be found in every province. In the United States, major populations of black bears are found primarily in the Rockies, the Great Lakes states, the Pacific Northwest and the mountains of California, the Appalachian mountains, New England, and some southern states such as Florida and Mississippi.

In their western U.S. and Canadian range, black bears share the ecosystem with grizzly bears, or at least, they once did. Where the ranges overlap, each species seeks a slightly different niche, and although black bears can approach the size of grizzlies, they rarely chose to confront this much more aggressive species. Black bears are denizens of the forest, and although they certainly can occasionally be seen feeding in the open, that is much more typical of the grizzly, which evolved for a more open-country existence.

It is probably the grizzly's predilection for open country that gave rise to its aggressive behavior, since a bear in the open doesn't have the option of scurrying up a tree when danger appears. In such instances, only the most aggressive bears survived, and they passed on that successful trait. Black bears, however, found that hiding in heavy cover, or slipping up a tree, was the best way to avoid trouble, and so shy bears also evolved.

That secretive behavior has helped the black bear survive in today's human-altered world. In contrast, the grizzly's aggressiveness nearly spelled its demise. Black bears routinely live today near humans. They may sneak in and tip over garbage cans, and they may eat some of the farmer's corn, but because they rarely pose a threat to humans, we tolerate them. We are much less tolerant of the grizzly, and its vastly reduced range reflects that intolerance.

Black bears may well be the most plentiful bear species left in the world.

OVERLEAF: The gentle nature of the black bear has helped it to avoid humans and confrontation, increasing the species' odds for survival in today's world.

CHAPTER TWO

Spring Beginnings

Spring brings new life to the forest.

SPRING IS A TIME FOR RENEWAL of living things, and it is no different for the black bear. Like all creatures that must deal with the rigors of winter, the black bear probably greets the dripping springtime woods with its own sense of relief. Even though it has spent most of the previous five or six months in hibernation, it hasn't survived without cost or dangers. Predators have been known to kill sleeping black bears. And even during hibernation, the body's fires must be fueled. The bear has lost a great deal of weight since late autumn when it entered its den, and springtime requires an awakening and a shift in metabolism.

Sows with cubs emerge from their dens later than males or sows without cubs.

If you've ever been roused too soon from a deep slumber, you may have some sense of just how a black bear feels after a winter-long sleep. There is that period of disorientation, during which you're not quite sure "what's up" or where you are. When you stand, muscles that were used to repose sometimes fail to follow your brain's lead—you're a bit wobbly. And of course, you're slow and awkward, unable to do anything quickly.

In the spring, when a black bear awakens, something similar occurs. Naturally, it is difficult to truly assess just how a bear feels, but researchers note a bit of "discombobulation" about a bear when it first arises. But, as with most things in life, there are exceptions. Bears can rouse quickly when need be.

I recall one incident when biologists for the Minnesota Department of Natural Resources moved in to anesthetize and relocate a bear that had chosen to hibernate near my home in Duluth. Afraid that bears that hibernated in town would then give birth to "city bears" that would later cause problems, these men decided to make this sleeping bear even sleepier, then move it to a den they had created for it far out of the city. Unfortunately, it didn't quite work as planned.

Crawling into the old, abandoned concrete culvert the bear had chosen for its den, the biologist gingerly prodded the bruin with a drug-filled syringe taped to the end of a pole. Only the man's feet protruded from the makeshift den as he prepared to deliver the shot.

"Pull me out, pull me out!" he suddenly yelled, his voice muffled by the tunnel. We grabbed his boots and yanked. As he appeared, so did the bear—inches behind

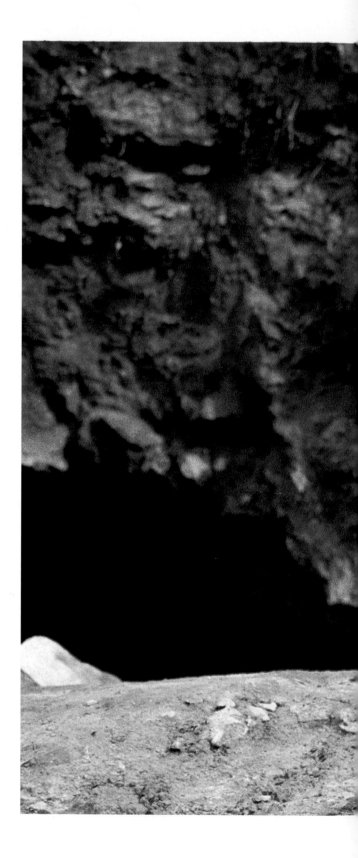

Upon emergence, black bears are often somewhat dazed and confused.

No one single factor determines when a bear awakens from its hibernation.

him—running at full tilt into the nearby winter woods. Obviously, this bear wasn't a deep sleeper and reacted swiftly.

Fortunately for all, he (a yearling male) finally slumped to the ground when the drug completed its job. When he awoke the next spring, he found himself in a much more natural setting, far out in the forest.

EMERGENCE

Days lengthen and nights shorten. Spring equinox arrives. The entire forest begins a new life. Plants and animals alike change condition. For some, like the deer and elk, it requires but a shift in territory, a movement to where the sun arrives early and the first spring foods sprout. Most predators, like the wolf, find they must shift from one prey species to another; from deer that had been easier to catch because of the winter's deep snows, to beavers or muskrats, since now the deer can easily flee.

For the black bear, it means throwing off the yoke of hibernation. When bears emerge from their dens depends largely upon where they live. Emergence is generally later in the spring in the North, and in some parts of the black bear's southern range, it can be as early as midwinter. For northern bears, most of whom were denned up by October, spring arrives sometime in late March or April, although they sometimes remain denned until early May. In mountainous areas, bears that have denned at high elevation emerge later than those at lower elevation.

The disparity in emergence times indicates that no one factor dictates the timing. Many things about wildlife behavior are influenced by photoperiod; that is, the amount of daylight hours in a day. For instance, a deer's antler growth is triggered by photoperiod, for the lengthening of days in turn triggers hormones that dictate antler production. Although environmental factors—the amount of food, for instance—or an animal's health can slightly modify such occurrences, they are relatively fixed in timing.

Such is not the case for the black bear's den departure. Photoperiod most likely plays a role, but in this instance, other factors appear to weigh equally. Much might depend upon the bear's health. If it went into the den in great shape with thick stores of fat, it is better able to delay emergence. But a hungry bear, a bear whose energy stores are depleted, must depart as soon as there is any chance of finding food.

In other cases, air temperature plays a role. If the bear is physically able to remain in the den, a delayed spring may encourage it to do so since there would be little outside to eat. In this instance it makes good sense for the bear to remain in hibernation with its internal "thermostat" turned down to conserve energy.

It is most likely that all these factors help determine a particular bear's emergence date. And that date will differ between bears even though they are geographically near each other, for no two bears have the same physiology.

There are other environmental factors that may cause one bear to emerge while another sleeps in. There have been numerous accounts of den flooding that has prompted bears to depart where they otherwise might have wished to remain. Melting snow or an odd midwinter rainstorm may seep into a bear's subterranean vault. There have been reports of flooded dens causing cub losses due to drowning or hypothermia induced by exposure to the cold water.

In some cases, especially if it is midwinter, black bears climb out, gather boughs or grasses, and return to the den to build up their bed's height so that they are above the water. If this isn't possible, they may search out a completely new site. If it is near spring, or in the South, they may choose to remain above ground and continue to sleep on an open bed of grass or sedge. And if spring is just around the corner, they may stay awake.

So although we can't say with certainty just which factor woke a particular bear this spring, we can make some pretty accurate generalized statements. In most instances, adult male bears depart the den first, mothers with cubs depart last (up to six weeks later), and subadult males and females emerge sometime in between.

It is interesting that the big male bear departs as early as he does. Usually, large adult males have a well-defined territory which they know intimately. This means they are masters at extracting its resources—they know where the best food sources are located and when they'll be available. This translates then into bears that go into winter in very good shape with large stores of fat, which also means that physiologically, they could remain in hibernation much longer. And while females sometimes return to their den for short periods even after emerging,

Although they may be curious about plant foods, newly emerged cubs depend almost entirely upon mother's milk.

males almost never do.

No doubt, the store of fat they retain that would have allowed a longer hibernation is equally critical to a successful early emergence (there have been cases of early-emerging bears starving to death before summer). At the time these males emerge, there really is very little to eat. Few plants, if any, have greened up. Insects are still inactive. Large males may be able to scrounge some carrion or pull down an old, winter-weary moose. But even meat protein is probably scarce during this period, since deer fawns and moose calves have yet to be born. So why get out and about so early?

Some researchers speculate that it is a reproductive advantage. Late spring or early summer is the black bear's breeding season, and male bears travel long distances to find their mates. It could be that this early emergence allows males to scout the area and to mark their territory. If so, it is just another one of the many examples where sexual dimorphism (males being larger than females) is important to a species' survival. In this case, the male's large size means he can cover long distances, taking advantage of this time period's meager and widely scattered foods. At the same time, he increases his odds of being a successful breeder and passing on his genes.

As the older boars emerge, females with cubs remain in their dens. If the mother is denning with the previous year's cubs—now called yearlings—she will emerge earlier than if she has given birth during the winter. Exposing this year's cubs to the cooler weather would needlessly decrease their chances of survival. A warm den and a nursing mother are great advantages.

Once the mother and cubs have emerged, energy consumption for all increases. Once out of hibernation, their metabolism speeds up. They make less efficient use of their stored energy, plus they now must counteract the vagaries of wind, rain, and late snows. With these additional demands, the mother bear still must maintain her own health and produce milk for her cubs, which is their sole source of nutrition at this stage. Staying in the den, then, is by far the best thing to do, and ages of natural selection have favored such behavior.

Teenage, or subadult, black bears emerge later than the males, but generally earlier than mothers with cubs. Subadults usually enter the den with less fat reserves than adult bears. They are less adept at finding good foods than are experienced adult bears, and because they are lower in the pecking order, are sometimes kept away from good food sources by dominant adults. By spring, they no longer have the energy reserves to maintain hibernation and must begin to feed. Staying in the den longer is neither the option nor advantage for them that it is for female bears with cubs.

When cubs emerge, they face for the first time a wonderful but sometimes hostile world. Their first year will be the most dangerous. From 1982 to 1995 a sample of 129 male cubs and 113 female cubs was studied by the Minnesota Department of Natural Resources. Its observations revealed that 22 percent of the male cubs disappeared within their first year, while 11 percent of the female

cubs vanished. The researchers speculate that these cubs died, but as yet have been unable to explain the higher mortality rate for male cubs.

FOOD GATHERING

When they emerge, black bears can be rather sleepy and appear lethargic. The physiologic miracles that allow for hibernation

Mother bears continue to lose weight as they produce milk for their cubs while themselves feeding on the often sparse foods of spring.

OVERLEAF: When they step into the new world for the first time, cubs will be about 4 weeks old and weigh about 8 pounds.

simply don't turn off overnight. While mature males may begin to wander their territory immediately, many younger bears, and especially females with cubs, tend to loiter in the neighborhood of their den for a week or two, even returning to it for naps. Some mothers may stay around the den for a month, and even bring fresh bedding into it.

When they don't return to the den, most bears create a series of day beds—often a pile of pine needles, leaves, and grass heaped up near the base of a tree in the vicinity of the denning site. Mothers frequently choose a particularly large tree for these nest sites so that their offspring can rapidly escape up it should danger appear.

If adult bears are lethargic at this time of year, cubs are a bundle of energy. They begin to tumble and play immediately upon discovering their new world, while mother watches carefully. All of a cub's nutrition comes from its mother's milk, and cubs will nurse until the middle of summer, so life is pretty carefree for them if she can remain healthy. And that's not always easy.

Even though black bears begin to feed almost immediately upon emerging, spring is not a time of abundance. Bears encounter a feeding deficit—the quality of the food is generally so low that no matter how much they eat, they usually continue to lose weight. This can become a serious matter because they've already lost considerable weight over the winter—up to a 30 percent weight loss for all bears, and as much as 40 percent for nursing females. The most vulnerable bears are the subadults who went into winter with less fat stores than their mature counterparts. April, May, and early June can prove to be dangerous and stressful times, and it is not unheard of for bears of all ages and both sexes to starve to death amidst a lush spring.

Why? While freshly sprouted forbs and grasses are at their nutritional peak, they still aren't sufficient to power a large bear. They swiftly harden and turn to indigestible cellulose as the plants mature. As discussed earlier, the gut of a bear is that of a carnivore—it is poorly adapted to digest vegetative matter. With a digestive tract too short to wring from a plant its full complement of nutrition, the bear can starve, or lose weight, even while eating nearly constantly. Remaining winter fat continues to play an important role in survival, and those bears without it can be in trouble. Protein in the form of insects is hard to find until summer really blossoms, and fruits, which are a staple later in the year, are months from ripening. Without digestible foods, a bear already underweight can starve, although the vast majority weather this lean period.

Some do this through hunting. At no time of the year is a black bear more of a predator than it is in the spring. Summer, with its hives, anthills, and stumps full of larvae, provides easily caught and highly nutritious insect protein. Typically, however, it takes weeks or a month of warm weather for these creatures to become active and lay eggs. Some bears simply can't wait that long.

While the bears are wandering about in search of food, white-tailed and mule deer, moose, and elk are giving birth. The offspring of all these members of the deer family share

Cubs are both curious and playful.
Their sharp little claws make them adept climbers.

a common survival strategy—the mother leaves her offspring in a well-hidden place so that she can move off to browse. Since she can't easily hide and simultaneously meet her own nutritional requirements (she's eating a lot so that she can produce milk for her offspring), which requires intensive browsing and grazing, and because she is visible and can attract predators, she hides her young.

The black bear is only a part-time predator.

The fawn or calf is left alone for up to 12 hours, with the mother returning infrequently to nurse it and move it to a new, odor-free site. These youngsters are well camouflaged, nearly scentless, and can remain motionless for hours on end—a practice known as "hider strategy." And because the deer and bear are often feeding on the same succulent new spring growth, all of them are in relatively close proximity to each other.

Given this scenario, it is no wonder that the intelligent and adaptable black bear has learned to hunt these defenseless young. In many parts of the country, black bears not only stumble across these fawns and calves, they routinely search, stalk, hunt, and kill them.

Black bears have also been noted catching birds on their nest, eating bird eggs, and in Florida, actually raiding alligator nests. Surprisingly, alligators defend their nests against all comers but slink away when a bear appears.

Fishing is another important spring predatory behavior. Across a broad section of the black bear's range, spawning runs of suckers occur just after emergence. Suckers spawn in small, shallow streams, making them easily caught by black bears. Although a black bear may only feed on fish for a brief period of time, it can be a significant factor in that bear's survival because the food is of such high nutritional quality.

But even if the black bear didn't catch the dead fish or animal, it usually won't pass it up. Those bears that emerge earliest can take advantage of winter-killed or stillborn cervids such as moose or deer, and this carrion can be a significant factor in an individual bear's survival.

Feeding on carrion is often portrayed as if it were luck or happenstance, but perhaps there is more to it than that. Wintering areas for deer, elk, and moose are often used for several generations. During a particularly bad winter, wintering areas can contain a large number of carcasses, frozen and fairly well preserved unless fed upon by other scavengers before a bear arrives. A large, smart bear that has chosen a territory overlapping a wintering area will also reap the benefit of the carcasses. In such a case you have to wonder if this is purely accidental, or if that territory was chosen and defended because such a food source would be present.

Even though such forays into scavenging or predation may be nutritionally significant, most of the feeding time of a black bear is spent searching for plant foods. Black bears frequently eat catkins—the sprouting flowers of trees, particularly the aspen—and the leaves themselves. Harvesting these treats takes skill and ingenuity. Some catkins can be had by climbing mature trees, but frequently they are out of reach far above on limbs too fragile to support the bear.

More often, black bears strip catkins from young trees using a clever technique. They stand on their back legs, reach forward with their front paws, and bend the main stalk of the tree down to where they can grab it with their jaws. Then the bear simply hangs by its teeth, using its weight to bend the tree to the ground, where it strips the leaves or catkins from the branches by drawing them through the gap between the fang and molar.

Other spring foods include the flower and leaves of the skunk cabbage, as well as grasses, sedge, and horsetail. These bears can and do partake of ants, which can be found even in spring by ripping open anthills. Once the bear has taken the top of the anthill off, the ants swarm to the surface, where the nubile tongue of the black bear awaits them.

Stumps frequently harbor colonies of insects—
a favorite food of black bears.

OVERLEAF: Depending on the size of their territory, bears may wander quite widely in search of food.

While spring may be a time of weight loss for adults, it is a period of growth for the cubs, which are still dependent upon mother's milk. Gradually, as summer nears, cubs start to test foods they see their mother eat. As they follow her around her territory, they not only learn which foods might be palatable, they also learn their home range, and where food and water can be found.

They must put on weight quickly. Emerging from the den at 4 to 8 pounds, a cub must reach 40 to 70 pounds in order to survive its first winter. Mother bears are taxed heavily by the demands of nursing cubs. Spring is tough enough for any bear, but she must not only preserve her own health, she must also create enough milk to ensure that her tumbling, squealing cubs continue to grow. These demands mean that female black bears are the most stressed members of the population, and their reproductive success is strongly tied to the quality and amount of food they obtain. Obviously, bears that have either inherited, or sought out, quality home ranges that meet their nutritional needs will survive to reproduce.

If spring has been kind, surviving black bears turn their attention to perhaps the only other thing that rivals food in interest and importance: reproducing.

THE MATING SEASON

Although the black bear's mating season isn't limited to spring—it can continue on into July—it certainly begins then, generally in late to mid-May. The majority of bears breed in June. It is one of the few times during the year when the otherwise secretive and solitary black bear seeks the company of other bears.

Cubs must reach 40 to 70 pounds of weight by autumn to have a chance to survive their first winter.

Black bears are relatively slow to reach sexual maturity. Females breed at a younger age than males—they can breed at 2½ years of age. This is the exception, though, not the rule, since the average age of first breeding is 3½, and it is not uncommon for females to have their first litter when they are 6 or 7, especially in the North. Males also are physically able to breed at around age 3, but

since males compete for mates, and these young males have neither the size nor experience to deal with larger, older males, they rarely get the chance to reproduce until they attain large size. For many males, this may mean waiting until they are 7 or more years of age.

Male black bears mate with as many females as they can during the brief mating season. Because its territory is much larger than that of a female, a mature male's range may overlap as many as a dozen—or even more—female ranges. During the course of his spring wandering, a male is constantly on the lookout for these females. Female black bears are in heat for about 3 weeks, but this length of time is deceptive. The male's opportunity to breed them will come only briefly, since a sow black bear's estrus—that time during which she is fertile and will allow him to mount her—is only 3 to 5 days in length. The wise old male then must locate and monitor the females that share his territory so that he is available when they are ready.

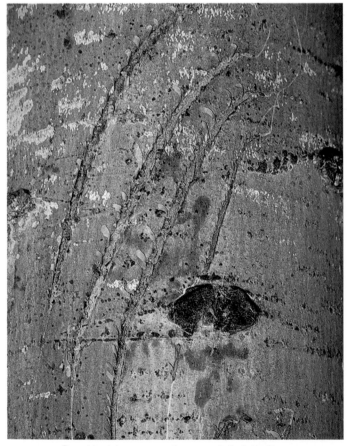

Boar black bears sometimes mark their territory by scratching trees with their claws.

Although young males sometimes do breed females when older males are either elsewhere in the territory or aren't present in the population, the larger, older males do most of the breeding. Black bears use a series of "bear trees" scattered along the trails of their territory to display their presence, both to other males and to prospective mates. These trees are recognizable by the furrowed scratches in the bark, generally at the maximum height the bear can reach, made by the male's claws. He may also bite at the tree. Black bears don't have scent glands like those a white-tailed buck uses to mark his antler rubs, but by rubbing themselves on their trees their scent is left behind.

During his search for a ready mate, a male bear eats very little. His sensitive sense of smell is checking the air currents for the distinct odor of females in heat, which is also revealed in the urine of female bears. If he smells a female and senses she is still nursing cubs, he will avoid her. Lactating female black bears do not come into heat, and so breed on an every-other-year schedule. Avoiding these females saves the male bear time and energy.

If a male discovers another male, either alone or already accompanying a female, he will attempt to drive the competitor away. There is an advantage to being large and strong in these cases, which is why the species is sexually dimorphic (males larger than females). Through the ages, natural selection has ensured that the biggest males breed, and they in turn pass on the genes for "bigness."

Contests between males can consist of mere woofing and posturing, during which the smaller bear is given a chance to turn and flee, or they can result in outright battles. Fights between males usually only occur when the combatants are about the same size. Usually short in duration, and seldom fatal, they can be quite intense and fierce, leaving one or both males with scars and other wounds.

While the males are on this breeding hunt, females in heat go about their foraging business. There is some evidence that females increase their speed as they travel around their home range so that they may be more likely to encounter a male. Eventually, a male will encounter a female's trail and begin following her.

If a female black bear isn't ready for the male, she will ignore him or even run away. The male will attentively follow her, waiting for her body chemistry to tell her that she is ready. Once she is in the middle of her

Boars follow sows until she is receptive to mating. Copulation lasts from 10 to 30 minutes.

estrous period, she will allow the male to approach her. Over the course of 1 to 4 days, they may mate several times.

Each mating lasts about 10 to 30 minutes. Mating actually stimulates ovulation (the release of an egg). Since female bears frequently mate with more than one male, successive encounters trigger the release of more eggs. Because of this, it is not uncommon for members of a litter to have been fathered by different males. This phenomenon provides genetic variability that is beneficial to the female since it helps to increase the odds of passing on her genes. Even if one of the fathers should prove to be genetically defective, it is unlikely all of them would be, and so one or more of her offspring would surely survive. This type of genetic variability is also beneficial to the species as a whole.

Once a female has completed her mating cycle she will not tolerate males near her, to the point of aggressiveness. She now must turn her attention to eating frequently—and eating well—in order to build up the fat reserves she'll need to give birth during hibernation and to produce milk for her cubs.

Bears have evolved a remarkable strategy that maximizes the odds of survival for both the female and any cubs that may be born. Whereas in humans and most other mammals, the fertilized egg (called a zygote) soon implants in the uterus to begin development, in black bears the development stalls after the cells have divided a few times. At this stage, the embryo (called a blastocyst) floats freely in the sow's uterus and does so for the entire course of the summer. Called embryonic delay, this stage of being "almost pregnant" has three distinct advantages.

First, it delays gestation so that the cubs will be born in January or February, which in turn means that they actually begin growing and nursing in the winter, and emerge in the spring. Such timing gives the little bears the maximum amount of growing time before they must face the rigors of their first winter, an important consideration because larger cubs have higher survival rates.

Second, it is a survival strategy that preserves the health and future reproductive potential of the female bear. Should the food crop fail, and the female enter autumn and winter at a low weight and in poor condition, the blastocysts will not attach to the uterus. She will simply absorb them. This relieves her of the stress of pregnancy and nursing, which, in her poor health, might otherwise be fatal to her and almost certainly to any cubs she might produce. Able to escape pregnancy, she increases her odds of living to breed at a time much more favorable to her and her future offspring.

Third, it frees a bear to concentrate on eating and putting on fat. Without delayed implantation, bears would need to mate in the fall in order to have a late-winter birth. Fall is too important a time, however, to "waste" on mating activity. As hibernators, black bears must devote their entire attention to feeding during those last months when foods ripen.

HOME TERRITORY

One other important behavior is tied to the mating season: the break-up of bear families. A sow with yearling cubs will now let

Males will fight for the right to mate with a female in estrus.

Females are very protective of their offspring.

them know that she will no longer tolerate their presence. The confused yearlings—now about 17 months old—are driven off by their aggressive mother or an aggressive male. Yearlings will stay for awhile in their mother's home range, and may even stay in each other's company for months. Eventually, the female yearlings will grow to inherit portions of their mother's range, and the mother will modify her range to accommodate them. Young males, however, will disperse to establish a new home territory, seeking a niche between ranges occupied by mature males. The dispersal of males probably evolved to help ensure that related bears don't breed together.

Of the two sexes, females are more territorial than males. Smaller in size, and slowed down by the responsibility of motherhood, females not only need to choose a territory wisely, they need to protect it. They will defend it by chasing off, and even fighting with, intruding female black bears. The reasons are obvious. All of her reproductive potential—she'll spend less than a quarter of her entire life alone—is linked inexorably with her health, which in turn is tied dramatically to how well she eats.

The size and shape of a territory will depend upon topography and the kinds of foods available.

The size of her territory will depend upon its location and the richness of food found therein—it could be as small as 3 square miles or as large as 10. Bear density (the total number of bears in the area) also influences the size and shape of a sow's territory. Over the span of her life, it will change little unless she needs to modify her movements to take advantage of new food sources or make room for female offspring.

Occasionally, black bears migrate out of their territory to utilize an important food only seasonally available elsewhere, such as a run of white suckers in a stream or abundant mast crops on a forested ridge. Female territories only rarely overlap those of other females, except in areas like Great Smoky Mountains National Park where abundant food seems to have led to less territoriality among the numerous female black bears.

While females have territories that they defend, male black bears aren't territorial. The area the male bear frequents in the course of a year is better described as a "home range." He does not defend this home range against other male bears, except when they are directly competing for a female in estrus.

OVERLEAF: Although black bears try to avoid fights among themselves, confrontation over territories or mates may leave an animal with wounds or scars, as in this case.

Boars generally stay out of each other's way at all other times, even if their home ranges overlap. However, the home ranges of males tend to overlap the territories of females much more frequently—perhaps even intentionally—in order for the male to be available for breeding. Males tend to stay out of the heart of a female's territory, though, except when pursuing her to mate.

It would be unwise for a male bear to compete with a female for the foods found within the female's range if she is tending to his own offspring. He'd be stealing food from their mouths, which would only serve to lower the odds of the successful passing on of his genes. Larger, without cubs, and freer to roam, a male bear can utilize foods that would be too widely dispersed for a mother with cubs, thus minimizing competition between him and his offspring or their mother.

Still, male bears aren't always concerned about the welfare of cubs. An unpleasant, but fairly common behavior, among black bears, is infanticide. There have been numerous cases where male bears have killed the new cubs of sows. Mother black bears clearly recognize the danger presented by boar bears, as evidenced by their propensity to build day beds near trees up which their cubs can escape. They also aggressively defend their cubs against males as well, even if the male is many times larger.

Why would male bears kill cubs? Researchers speculate that this is yet another example of the imperative animals feel to pass on their genes. As noted earlier, lactating females do not come into heat and therefore are unavailable for breeding purposes. But if a sow loses her cubs, she will shortly come into heat.

It is the mother's responsibility to keep cubs safe.

The cub-killing male will then be able to breed her. Some of these incidents occur well into summer, and females have been known to have been bred successfully into September.

Although it would be difficult to determine without long and careful observation, or without genetic analysis, it would seem that boars might be more likely to kill cubs if they were the offspring of another male, as is the case with lions. There doesn't seem to be a genetic advantage to periodically killing your own descendants.

ON INTO THE SUMMER

From their dazed emergence from an icy winter, to the heated excitement of the mating season, black bears in spring face numerous challenges. It may seem strange that a season that for so many animals is one of birth and renewal should be the most stressful for the black bear, yet it is. Winter, by comparison, was easy.

Summer, however, is a time of relative ease. Foods become increasingly more plentiful. Energy consumption lessens for all bears as the weather warms, particularly for the female, whose cubs begin to depend less and less on her milk.

But summer in bear country is often short. And black bears know it. There will be little time to waste.

Except when fish or animals are easy to catch, black bears eat mostly plants and insects.

OVERLEAF: With summer abundance comes a need for relaxation, especially for yearlings.

CHAPTER THREE

Summer Sojourn

Summer is short in black bear country.

ALL THE THINGS WE HUMANS appreciate about summer—the warm weather, the abundance of life, the ripening of foods, the long daylight hours— are things that the black bear also finds to its liking. And all the things that we don't like about the summer woods—the eruption of biting insects or the thickness of the forest undergrowth that hinders travel—are things that pester the black bear, too. By and large, summer is an easy time for the bear—a time for cubs to grow and learn, and the beginning of its feeding binge for weight gain.

Summer brings warm weather, new foods—
and annoying insects.

In fact, there is little else for the black bear to do during this time of year than eat and learn. Cubs, though still somewhat dependent upon mother's milk, are taking their first tentative bites of the foods they see her eat. Wandering in her wake, they are also learning about their home territory, about cross-country travel, about woods and waters. Even about humans and their homes, roads, and garbage. For these little bears, having just come into the world with spring, everything is brand-new.

Late spring and early summer is the mating season for black bears. By the end of June, unless a sow were to lose her cubs to starvation or predation and therefore come into estrus, all the cub-less female black bears will have been bred. Because of the possibility of infanticide by adult male bears, those females with cubs continue to guard them jealously. As discussed earlier, male bears sometimes kill cubs (in some areas of the black bear's range, infanticide due to marauding males is the largest cause of cub mortality) so as to induce the female to come into estrus—something that can't happen as long as she's producing milk. Because of this, mother black bears rarely take their cubs far from the protection of a tree. No matter the cause of her alarm, a short grunt will send the cubs scurrying up a tree so that she is able to assess the danger and defend them if needed.

While black bears can often be seen feeding in an open meadow or forest clear-cut, those farthest from the forest's edge are generally males or females without cubs. When mother bears with cubs do feed in such surroundings, they'll generally stay near the edge. They may even send their cubs up a tree even though danger isn't present, to be

By summer, cubs are becoming less dependent
upon mother's milk, and begin to sample different foods.

Black bears that fail to avoid human contact frequently end up in trouble,
with a large percentage eventually being killed.

able to venture into the open for food that may be present there.

Evolution has dictated this behavior. Generations of black bears that did flee up trees survived, while those that stood their ground—whether against the more aggressive open-ground grizzly or other predators—lost their cubs. Natural selection has chosen black bears for a more secretive and escape-oriented behavior, and that strategy has served the species well.

It continues to work well even in this human-altered world, for the black bear's inherent shyness allows it to live very near to humans. Those black bears that don't challenge people and their dogs, that stay away from garbage cans and homes, and that scurry quickly away from roadsides are the ones that live the longest and therefore will reproduce the most times. Our world keeps reinforcing the black bear's natural proclivity for secretiveness.

Weather Influences

Evolution also dictated that the black bear be equipped to survive cold weather. Animals in the tropics generally store fat internally or in areas of the body that don't

Black bears have been known to visit water simply for its cool relief.

interfere with their ability to cool themselves. In contrast, cold-weather mammals like the black bear store fat on the outside, just beneath the skin. In addition to serving as a storehouse for energy, fat so located also provides a thick layer of insulation against the cold.

There is some disadvantage to this in the summer, of course. But for most black bears, summers are short, and the cold months last as long as nine or ten months of the year. And they do have some adaptive behaviors to help offset the discomforts of summer heat.

First and foremost is the ability to shed fur. The summer molt sees the near-complete loss of the woolly undercoat that served the bear so well over the winter, as well as the replacement of the longer, outer guard hairs. Black bears can look pretty bedraggled by June and July, but by autumn their new, sleek coat is in place.

In most animals, the trigger that begins the shedding or growing of fur is photo-period. Lengthening days stimulate the pituitary gland, which induces chemical secretions that tell the animal it is time to shed. A similar process, this time involving

the shortening of daylight hours in the autumn, stimulates hair growth. While there is no concrete evidence at this time to indicate that photoperiod is the most important factor in a black bear's molting process, it is the most likely cause.

Molting is a gradual process. At no time do black bears lose so much fur that they are left unprotected against the elements or biting insects. The bear's coat, except around the muzzle, is thick enough even in summer to fend off most biting bugs, but those insects that burrow, like ticks and black flies, find their way through the fur. It is not uncommon to see black bears with clusters of blood-engorged ticks attached at the ears or other areas of the head where the fur is thin enough to provide easy access.

In addition to the molting process, behavioral changes help the black bear to adjust to warm weather. On truly hot days, bears will restrict their movement to the coolest hours, or even become nocturnal. The warmest hours will be spent in the shade of a tree or cliff, where they make day beds of grass and leaves. Sows with cubs will locate these beds at the base of escape trees. These circular beds look much like those made by deer and are dismissed as such by the casual observer who hasn't stooped for an examination to look for black fur. Researchers have even noted a few instances where black bears, during extreme heat, climb back into their winter dens, where the subterranean hollows continue to capture coolness.

Black bears also like the water. While they frequently swim across lakes and streams to reach foods, they also swim apparently just for relief from heat and insects. Researchers like Dr. Lynn Rogers in Minnesota, observing bears in warm weather, have noted many such midday dips during which the bear did nothing but cool itself, with no travel or feeding behaviors linked to it.

Black bears have even been observed using their broad, flat paws to dip water, which they then pat on the top of their head where it can evaporate. The effect is the same as when a human hiker dips a bandanna in a creek and then drapes it over the head or ties it around the neck. Convection from the evaporating water provides soothing, cool relief.

Bears have also been seen wallowing in mud or low areas in wet bogs. Such wallowing probably also provides heat relief, and a coat of plastered mud may possibly serve as protection against biting insects.

Unless hot weather dictates a halt, black bears wander widely each day in search of food. Bears in undisturbed parts of the United States and Canada have a routine remarkably similar to a human's—asleep soon after dark and up at dawn—a pattern known as diurnal. But where they frequently run into humans, black bears can become almost completely nocturnal—that is, they are active during the night. Animals that are active primarily at dawn and again at dusk (as are some black bears) are known as crepuscular. Depending upon the situation and location, black bears will adopt any or all of these behaviors.

Each summer the black bear sheds its thick winter coat.

OVERLEAF: Black bears tend to avoid each other except around food sources or during mating. When they do encounter each other, dominance is largely dictated by size.

Social Structure

Because the summer forest is thick, bears frequently utilize a network of trails that are created simply by repeated use. These become increasingly dense near concentrations of foods, like berry patches. Bears that share trails also share information with each other, whether they know it or not. Droppings and urine along the trail will tell other passing bears many things—like whether or not the bear that went before it was a male or a female, and if a female, whether she was in heat. They may even be alerted to food sources of which they would otherwise be unaware by smelling berries or fish in the scat, and then backtracking to find the source.

But perhaps most important is the ability to avoid other bears by having sensed their presence on the trails. Young males seek to avoid dominant boars, and females with cubs want to elude them too. Having scented them along the trail, the bear can make an informed choice about whether or not to proceed.

But bears don't always choose to avoid each other. Foods have a tendency to ripen in one area before they do in another, as with berries on a south slope or hazelnuts in the shade. Inevitably, where bear densities are high enough, these temporary concentrations of food will also create temporary concentrations of black bears. Although solitary creatures much of their lives, bears do need to tolerate each other when such situations arise, and so have developed means of telegraphing their position in a hierarchy.

Hierarchies are an extremely important part of a species' success story. Without them, chaos would rule. Animals would spend time

Aggressive snarling is an obvious clue to a bear's disposition at the moment.

fighting with each other, rather than eating or caring for young. Injuries, and even death, could occur in the short run, and in the long run, even without injuries, the energy wasted in fighting would detract from their feeding, which would leave them in poor shape to face winter or a breeding season. All of these negatives result in decreasing a species' success, and so it should come as no surprise that natural selection has nurtured the evolution of behavioral displays or clues that keep conflict to a minimum.

Black bears, although only part-time carnivores at this point in their evolution, were total carnivores at their evolutionary roots—which at one point shared a common canid ancestor with the dog and wolf. Some of these canid behaviors can still be seen today in how bears deal with each other, with one exception. The most obvious clue to canid status is the tail position—up and out is dominant, tucked is submissive. Bears have short tails that are unfit for such display, but they nonetheless seem to have the dog's and wolf's ability to assess body language.

Sometimes, the ability to evaluate body language isn't even necessary. Rank can often quickly be determined by size. In general, the bigger the bear, the higher it will be in the dominance hierarchy. Therefore, smaller bears (unless they're mothers with cubs) give way in crowded circumstances to larger bears. But the real problem comes when near-equals meet or when a mother must face a large male. It is at times like these that being able to evaluate an opponent's intentions through his or her body language becomes important. The struggle for food is critical, yes. But little advantage is gained if one is injured. Bears rely on the ability to "best guess" what their potential opponent might do. They carefully watch the head, ears, and posture.

In these cases, each animal watches the other for clues to its rank and disposition. Upright ears indicate alertness, while flattened ears seem to mean two things (and

Body language can show many dispositions—
not only aggression.

perhaps only the bears know which one they mean at the time!): look out, I'm charging; or, help, I'm frightened.

Posturing bears display a truly canine behavior, each circling while watching the other out of the corner of an eye. Such a position allows the animal to whirl quickly to charge its opponent or to whirl away equally fast should it decide to flee. Noises, such as grunting and the clicking of its teeth, are also clues to a bear's state of excitement.

Through the use of these tools bears tend to avoid most conflicts. Even if it comes to the point where one charges the other, these charges often break off before full contact is made. When posturing or charging works, neither bear is the worse for the challenge and each can resume its routine. The victor, of course, will take the spoils of food for his or her effort.

Sometimes, though, posturing or bluffing isn't enough. Fights do occur, but they tend to be rare, for even the victor risks injury and thus its own long-term ability to forage for itself. In black bear country, it is a rare situation that warrants that risk. A few quick cuffs by the more dominant bear may be enough to send the challenger fleeing. Sometimes, though, it isn't always the bigger bear that wins. Females with cubs can be ferocious in their defense, and have been known to attack and drive off male bears over twice their size.

It isn't certain whether this "bear language" crosses bear species. Black bears often live near grizzlies, and while black bears tend to avoid grizzlies whenever possible, inevitably they bump into each other in

a berry patch. As a rule, black bears give way, but there have been instances where large black bears have challenged (and driven away) smaller grizzlies. After all, both bears are similarly equipped physically. It is generally the black bear's more timid behavior that reduces conflict. As a bear grows large, however, its timidity may be tempered by its status within the bear population—

Although bears would rather not fight, some dominance battles do occur, and they can leave an old bear scarred.

large is good in the bear world. In such cases, a big boar black bear may be reluctant to give way to a small grizzly just because of the latter's species.

We humans would do well to study these clues bears use to evaluate each other and apply them when we encounter black bears. Although black bears could be dangerous if they wanted to be—they are, after all, large, powerful animals with sharp claws and sharp teeth—that same evolved "flee" strategy that makes them a success in general means they would rather run from than fight with a human. Researchers have even been able to take bawling cubs away from females without being attacked, even though the mother made some bluff charges before backing down.

It's interesting to note that while a black bear is far, far less likely to attack a human than is a grizzly bear, when attacks do occur, the black bear is more likely to kill the human than is the grizzly. This seems to be due to two factors: grizzlies are aggressive because of their "fight rather than flee" survival strategy, but once the enemy is down, they often leave it alone.

Black bears, however, rarely attack humans at all, but when they do it seems to be a pure predatory attack—in other words, they don't grab a human because they feel threatened, but because they are hungry. Because of this, unless the human fights back violently, black bears generally continue to attack until they've killed their "meal."

Experts from agencies like state game and fish departments, the Forest Service, or the Park Service recommend you do whatever you must to defend yourself if attacked by a black bear. In contrast, many of these same people recommend that if a grizzly attacks, you play dead. In the latter case, the point being made to the grizzly is that you aren't the threat it perceived you to be, and the sooner that point is made to the bear, the greater the odds of your survival.

That said, black bears should not be thought of as dangerous animals. The potential is there, but the desire isn't. Rather than fearing a woodland encounter with a black bear, one would be better advised to fear the drive to and from that camping trip or outing, which is thousands of times more dangerous statistically.

FOOD OPTIONS

Mostly, human and black bear encounters are in the "nuisance" category: tipping of garbage cans, raiding apple trees or beehives, or stealing food from campers. Bears that perpetrate such petty offenses are often dealt with as though they had committed a felony—nuisance black bears are often killed. Many of these situations could have been avoided had people merely stored their food or garbage properly, and taken measures to dissuade bears. Frequently, bears repeat these nuisance behaviors because they have been rewarded for their thievery by getting food. Campers in particular can do much to keep black bears from becoming panhandlers and thieves by storing food in a locked vehicle or by hanging it in a tree when in the backcountry.

Serving as wilderness rangers in northern Minnesota's Boundary Waters Canoe Area

Black bears rarely pose a threat to humans, although it is always wise to be cautious in their presence.

Black bears have routes that they travel to and from regular food sources.

Wilderness, my wife and I not only had the opportunity to observe black bears around our cabin, but to monitor their behavior around the human visitors that paddled their way into our territory. Most of these encounters took place at night or in the early morning, and they almost always involved the bears' search for food, which the campers sometimes made too readily available.

These bears seemed to have a regular route that they traveled each week, and we could track (and therefore even predict) which campsites would be visited next simply by monitoring which campsites had

already been hit and when. Bear encounters near those campsites along the Basswood River seemed particularly easy to predict, since the bears would work their way west down the river. It seemed it took about a week or so for them to make the journey from Upper Basswood Falls to Lower Basswood Falls, each night visiting a handful of campsites. The number of sites they visited, and the number of days it took to complete their "route," depended upon whether their raids were successful. If they found food at the first site, they'd retreat into the forest to consume the meal. If they were

Black bears are not afraid of water and are capable swimmers.

thwarted by well-hung packs or dissuaded by a well-aimed rock on the rump, they'd move on down the river.

On a number of occasions, we saw a black bear swimming across the river or nearby Crooked Lake, cruising along like a Labrador retriever. In every instance we observed this, the bear was heading directly for a distant campsite. Often, campers who chose an island campsite did so under the mistaken belief that they need not worry about bears. Believing that, they were either particularly sloppy about hanging their packs or didn't bother to do so at all. The intelligent black bear learns quickly, and a few hundred yards of water, across which is wafting the odor of bacon, eggs, and flapjacks, proves merely to be an enjoyable swim.

Curiously, these island-hopping bear raids took place mainly in the full light of day, whereas most mainland raids took place at night. It could be that even bears don't relish swimming in the dark or during a cool night. And as it happened, many of these campsites were abandoned during the day while the occupants were out fishing or otherwise recreating. With no one there to drive the bear off, it was an easy raid.

OVERLEAF: Black bears are masters at finding and utilizing the food sources within their home range.

For it is food that is on the black bear's mind all summer long. And if they can get human food, they'll take it. But they sure don't need it. The summer woods are lush with many kinds of foods.

Early in the summer, as the sap is rising in the trees, bears frequently strip trees of their bark to get at the sapwood, or cambium layer. This soft, white layer is high in sugar and is 90 percent water. Black bears seem to prefer coniferous trees such as pines, firs, spruce, and cedar. In some parts of their range, this behavior gets black bears in trouble when they visit an industrial forest to dine on trees commercial foresters had planted for harvest.

Other parts of live trees that are consumed by black bears are the catkins and buds, as well as newly emerged leaves. Although primarily a spring behavior, this type of feeding continues into early summer as well, as long as trees are in the early stages of leafing out.

Where black bears live in the mountains, they may follow summer up the slope, since it comes later at higher elevations. And they may even then move from the south side (which receives more sun, and thus has an earlier "summer") to the north side (to which warmth comes later) to take advantage of the budding of trees as well as the sprouting of other vegetation, which is then at its nutritious best.

But dead trees provide food, too, for they frequently harbor stores of insects. Fallen trees in particular are important to bears, for as they rot on the ground, the decaying process provides natural heat. Insects lay their eggs in this warmer rotting wood, and in black bear country, a shredded fallen tree is a

As the summer progresses, ripening fruits become a favorite food.

Stumps and logs frequently hide nests of insects, a high-protein food delicacy for black bears.

sure sign that a black bear has been at work searching for grubs and larvae.

No black bear ever passes up the opportunity to swat an anthill so that it can lick up the swarming ants as they rise to the surface to defend their home. And even wasp nests aren't immune to a bear attack, despite the fact that wasps are much more able to defend their home than are ants.

Winnie-the-Pooh with his head stuck in a honey jar may be a character in a children's story, but it is based on truth, for black bears love honey. And will endure countless bee stings to get at a store of it in a hollow tree. Where beekeepers and bears share the same countryside, attacks on commercial hives can cause considerable damage and financial loss.

Summer to the black bear heading toward autumn is like a roller coaster ride just clearing the top of a rise and speeding toward the bottom. As black bears emerge in spring, they've lost much weight, and spring foods don't help much. They continue to lose weight into early summer, when they clear that rise. Then, in full blossom of herbs and fruits, the bear's feeding binge rolls on rapidly toward autumn. As each

The bear's digestive system is poorly designed for digesting fruits.

preferred plant ripens, bears will single-mindedly feed on it, taking full advantage of the plenitude. As one plant wanes, another waxes.

By the middle of summer, blueberries, in a good year, are plentiful. They are followed quickly by raspberries. Other choice berries are huckleberries, chokecherries, blackberries, and pin cherries. Apples and wild plums ripen. Black bears may travel great distances to utilize these foods—often well outside of their home range.

With their mobile lips and tongue, the bears move from one ripening cluster of berries to another, eating huge quantities. Have you ever seen purple scat? You will if you follow black bears around during blueberry season. And after eating apples, their droppings resemble apples chopped in a blender. Despite their taste for these fruits, it is clear that black bears are poorly equipped to process them but manage to gain enough nutrition and sugar to make eating them worthwhile.

Unless there has been a late frost, which can freeze the flowers of fruit and cause a complete crop failure, by the end of summer black bears have replaced much of

It takes a lot of food resources to feed a mother and three hungry cubs.

their lost weight. Cubs are less dependent upon mother's milk and are eating the fruits and insects alongside her. They, too, must fatten up for their first winter, which they will spend with their mother in hibernation. The lessons they've learned during the course of the summer by following their mother's example are the sole source of their learning.

Still playful and only about 30 pounds, late summer bear cubs are quick to flee up a tree at their mother's warning or scolding. But they've gotten through their own most dangerous period, and have only the short months of autumn to fatten up and enjoy before they reach the relative safety of the winter den.

OVERLEAF: Late summer cubs weigh about 30 pounds, but must still gain more weight in the autumn if they are to survive winter.

CHAPTER FOUR

Fall Is
for Food

Autumn warns of winter's coming.

AUTUMN IS TO BLACK BEARS as the holiday season is to most humans—a time for rapid weight gain. Nothing in the bear's life during this period, other than immediate survival for itself or its cubs, is more important than the quest for food.

In fall, the black bear's sole enterprise is weight gain.

Hard mast, such as these nuts, is an important source of fats and protein.

NUTS VERSUS BERRIES

As the first cool days of autumn replace the heat of summer, black bears increase both their wanderings and the number of hours per day spent in eating. It is a binge, the likes of which is seldom rivaled in nature. With the shortening of days and the first frost, the black bear's entire metabolism gears up for weight gain.

As summer wanes, photosynthesis ceases in many plants, causing the brilliant colors that endear this season to us. As well, some of the green vegetation favored by black bears begins to wither. Early-ripening fruits, like blueberries and raspberries, have all been consumed or have dropped from the vine. But all is not lost, for the autumn forest is the time for the ripening of fall crops and of great harvest.

Although black bears will partake of other foods during this period, their main dietary staple is mast—both hard mast and soft mast. Hard mast is composed of fat-rich nuts such as acorns, beechnuts, pine nuts. Availability is dependent upon geographical location, as well as on how well one tree species' nut production fared in comparison to others, since it isn't unusual for different

Soft mast, such as these fruits, is full of sugars and carbohydrates.

species to produce abundant crops cyclically.

At one time the eastern black bear was deluged in autumn with chestnuts, a much-favored bear food. Unfortunately, this tree is near extinction, largely because of disease brought to America from Japan. Thankfully, the many species of oak trees are not threatened, and their nuts have served as a suitable replacement. In fact, where oak trees are rare because of the climate, but where local microclimates allow small stands to flourish, black bears will travel great distances to find these trees and their nuts.

In the West, pine nuts must do instead of acorns. Black bears have been seen with forelimbs and chest caked with pine sap, having spent so much time in the trees gathering nuts.

Soft mast includes the fall-ripening berries, such as the succulent fruits of the mountain ash, apples, or buffalo berries. Although these fruits are not as rich in fats as are nuts, they still play an important role, especially for black bears in regions where nuts are less common. In those places, black bears tend to den later because it takes them longer to store up fat. They also tend to be smaller, and become sexually mature at a later age, so great is the difference in the nutritional value of nuts and berries.

Berries and bears seem to have a symbiotic relationship. First, the bear obviously benefits by eating the berries, although it is careful not to chew them too much because that would mash the seeds. Many berry seeds are slightly toxic and, if crushed, could release the toxins and sicken the bear. If the seeds aren't crushed during the chewing process, they pass through the bear's system whole. That saves the bear some discomfort, but it also benefits the berries.

The black bear's digestive system somehow modifies the seed in a manner which increases its germination rate. Studies have shown that seeds so processed in a black bear have 2 to 3 times the germination rate of seeds that merely dropped to the ground. And of course, the bear serves as the delivery vehicle, depositing the seeds in its fecal matter as it travels, perhaps introducing them to new and fertile soils they might otherwise never have reached.

FAT STORAGE

The black bear's feeding binge isn't due solely to the sudden availability of these foods; it is also due to an irresistible, innate urge. At other times of the year, black bears will stop eating when satiated, but in the autumn, there seems to be no end to their hunger. They will eat as long as they are awake, and sleeping hours are often cut short. For they know, at least biologically, that there will be plenty of time to sleep very, very soon.

This behavior is known by biologists as "hyperphagia" and is characterized by excessive

The appetite of a black bear in autumn is insatiable.

eating. It is controlled by biological changes over which the bear has no control. Chemical changes to its blood signal the onset of hyperphagia, and a return to normal blood chemistry will signal its end. But during the period in between, the weight gain of black bears is phenomenal.

It is not unusual, for instance, for a bear's caloric intake to increase from about 8,000 calories per day (average human intake is about 2,000 per day) to over 20,000. For this to happen, the black bear must eat nearly 3 times as much food during its waking hours as it did in the previous months. A large male bear might put on 200 pounds in just 2 months! Bears in such prime condition appear obese. Their bodies are caked with fat, and they ripple when they walk. The human equivalent of such a weight gain would make it difficult for us to walk and would put a strain on our heart. But black bears remain swift and energetic, thanks to their powerful build and body chemistry.

Apparently, once the bear has stored enough fat to sufficiently carry it through the winter, the hyperphagia shuts down and the bear begins to look for a denning site. The specific trigger for this behavioral change remains undiscovered by biologists.

Although autumn seems like a season of plenty, it is nonetheless a critical time of the year for black bears, for if they enter the winter in poor condition, survival is reduced. There aren't any second chances. Crop failures at this point, or an early and lasting snow, could put many bears at risk.

SUCCESSFUL REPRODUCTION

A lack of food this year can even affect next year's bears. The amount of fat a female carries also influences her reproductive success. Since black bears mate in the spring, the embryos, only barely developed, float freely in a female's uterus for the entire summer. But after the fall binge, should she have adequate stores of fat, the cells implant themselves on the uterus walls. In late November or early December, she quite suddenly becomes pregnant. Without food, however, she absorbs these cells. And even if the eggs do implant, just how much fat the sow has stored will influence the birth weight of her cubs, a factor that will influence her offspring's survival not only in their first year, but for every year of their lives.

A mechanism which is likely chemical in nature, and which is related to her fat stores, stimulates the embryos or uterus, causing implantation. The five-month delay has likely evolved around the bear's hibernation behavior.

With mating occurring in the late spring and early summer, bears take advantage of the time of year when energy can be expended upon the rituals of reproduction. Consider that a male bear must search widely for females. And should the female not be ready to mate, she must defend herself against amorous suitors. Both of these behaviors can be time-consuming and energy-intensive. But the main mating month of June is a time when there are fewer foods, and so it becomes a time that bears can "spare" for the mating game.

In autumn, bears eat 3 times more calories per day than they did in summer.

OVERLEAF: If she's been successful at weight gain, the mated female's embryos will implant on her uterus wall.

If bears were to mate in the autumn, as do most spring-birthing mammals, they would have to divert energy and time away from feeding. This would tax their ability to put on enough weight to survive hibernation. Thus, delayed implantation becomes a marvelous way to utilize both the bear's time and its surrounding resources.

There is yet one other advantage to this

Black bears mate in the spring so they can spend the autumn attaining the fat needed for hibernation.

system of delayed implantation for female black bears. Should the berry or nut crop fail, and food be insufficient for optimal weight gain, her embryos would simply fail to implant. She would then be spared the rigors of gestation and nursing, chores that might be beyond her physical means. Not only would her health or survival have been threatened, but those conditions would have meant underweight and poorly nourished cubs.

In the long view that nature so frequently takes, it is better for the individual female bear, and for the species itself, that she forego reproduction one year and instead marshal her strength for the future and better times for reproducing. As previously mentioned, the primary factor in the failure of embryo implantation is a lack of proper nourishment. Unless the bear is injured or sick and so unable to properly feed itself, undernourishment is usually due to a lack of food resulting from a berry or nut crop failure. And since these crop failures frequently occur in a fairly large area, what has triggered a failure to implant in one bear sow may very well have triggered the same response in other female bears of the region.

The crop failure, then, is sometimes mirrored by a "cub" failure—years when most of the sows in an area have failed to reproduce, followed by a year when they all reproduce. The effects can be passed on to the next generation when their female offspring, most of which will have all come to breeding age at the same time, produce their first litters all in the same year.

This phenomenon has been observed in varying degrees in several parts of North

America, and is called "reproductive synchrony." Of course, this is a trend, not a hard rule, or there would be years when there were no cubs at all. Even in years of bad crops, it is likely that some bears successfully implant and give birth, and although most of the second generation will come into estrus for their first time together, there always will be those who mature early or late, eventually erasing the effects of the synchrony of their mothers.

If the female has been successful in finding the food she needs, implantation will occur. Scientists speculate that implantation takes place in response to photoperiod—in this case the shortening of day length. Because the day length is the same for all the females in the same geographic region, so is the approximate implantation date. And so will be the birthing date, which, throughout most of the black bear's range, occurs from mid-January to early February. Each female responds to photoperiod similarly from year to year, and so each of her litters in subsequent years is likely to be born within days of the others. It really is a quite amazing chronology.

SEARCH FOR FOOD

Fall feeding is marked by wide wanderings, although this too is a balancing act. Bears must not wander excessively if there is little hope of finding food, since they could easily burn more calories in the search than they might take in once they reached the food source. This is where their keen memories play an important role.

Having followed their mother to a food source during their first year with her, cubs retain a mental map of the route to that place, which they can use once on their own. In places where acorns are rare, such as the Canadian Shield country, black bears will travel over 100 miles to reach a stand of nut-rich hardwoods. In these cases, the journey is well worth it calorically, for just a few days of eating such oil- and fat-rich nuts not only

Inquisitive cubs have been known to look anywhere for food.

replaces the energy lost in the migration, but also adds important pounds.

Bears have a distinct advantage over other nut eaters like wild hogs, wild turkeys, and deer. Black bears can climb to reach the nuts before they fall. But once the nuts are on the ground, other animals often beat them to the treasure. Black bears have been known to climb two or three stories into sturdy trees to get at nuts, and there are records of "bear nests" built in trees to facilitate aerial nut or berry gathering.

Jamming or bending branches into a crotch of the tree or a fork in a large branch, black bears create a platform that provides a sturdy base from which to browse. This also frees a paw or two from clutching branches for safety reasons to pull branches down to their waiting mouth. Black bears will also gnaw off branches that defy bending—up to 3 or 4 inches in diameter—and drop them to the ground. Then they descend to consume the harvest of nuts.

These movements, in addition to being fairly long in distance, can be rather long in duration, up to two months in length. Males seem to wander most widely, followed by females without cubs, but even those with cubs aren't averse to long journeys, especially in years when food is scarce.

This "fall shuffle," as it has been termed by some researchers, serves yet another purpose. During this time, yearling males, now on their own for the first time, combine these trips with their need to disperse. Such dispersals serve the purpose of removing the young male bears from their mother's home range. This avoids the possibility that they will mate with their mothers or female siblings (which take up residence, when they mature, in ranges adjacent to their mother).

These young males are both "on the move" and inexperienced, and so face a very high mortality rate caused by a number of factors. Bear hunting season in many places is also in the autumn, which can be the downfall of many young males. Others succumb to dangers they've never encountered before, such as roads. Still others are shot while searching for food by tipping over garbage cans or raiding gardens. In places where black bear country is also farm country, ripening corn is an almost irresistible lure to the bruins, which can do an impressive amount of damage to a crop of standing corn.

When Food Is Scarce

The most serious threat to black bears, though, is a mast failure. It isn't unheard of for tree species, even without a catastrophic drought or other environmental factors, to have lean years in berry or nut production. For some species, it's a three- or four-year cycle. A late frost, which isn't all that uncommon in the northern part of the black bear's range, can kill the flowers of berry plants just as they are germinating, and so halt berry production completely. That means that not every autumn provides black bears with the foods they need.

Indeed, in 1985, a hazelnut and berry failure in northern Minnesota sent hundreds of bears south from the Canadian Shield country north of Lake Superior. These hungry, wandering bears, upon reaching the big lake, were funneled south and west by its

Where acorns aren't available, pine nuts are an important food item.

shores until they ended up in my home city of Duluth.

That year, black bears were everywhere, not just in the rural or suburban surroundings, but wandering even into the downtown area and busy industrial port. They were visible during the day as well as at night. On some mornings, worried parents stood guard over their children at school bus stops while a mother bear and her cubs sat above in the branches of an old tree, waiting for all the excitement to die down so they could resume their foraging.

Many bears were trapped and relocated by the Minnesota Department of Natural Resources. Many others stayed the winter, by denning up in this forested city's back corners. And dozens more were shot and killed as nuisance bears. Driven by their uncontrollable hunger and deprived by nature of their accustomed food source, these black bears ate everything they could get their paws on—apples in backyard orchards, corn from garden plots, birdseed from the many bird feeders, garbage whenever they could get it and, at least in one instance, most of a 50-pound sack of dog food when yours truly forgot to shut the garage door one night.

For years afterward, even though natural food crops seemed sufficient, bear encounters in the city in the autumn were frequent. It is likely that the cubs that followed their mothers to town in their first autumn simply accepted that trip as the way an autumn forage was supposed to be. Since most only spend one autumn with their mother, and since that autumn was spent at a garbage can in the city rather than in the woods at a stand of oak

Young bears learn their way through the forest to food sources from following their mothers.

trees, the young bears not only were imprinted on the temptations of the big city, but had been denied the opportunity to imprint on the patches of natural food they might otherwise have visited.

These kinds of years, however, are not the rule. In a good year, mother and cubs will have found what they need to get fat enough for winter. Males and females without cubs have an even easier time of it, for they don't have rambunctious young ones to attend to and can devote more time to feeding. In addition, due to the demands of nursing through the summer, energy that might otherwise have gone into fat storage has been used for milk production. The female with cubs enters the winter at a slightly more precarious state than most other bears.

By the time October rolls around, most bears are not only fat, they have grown a new, lush and oily coat of fur. Nature has programmed the bear to develop all that it needs to survive its most miraculous feat and the most demanding season of the year. Eating tapers off as the chemical urges sent by its blood chemistry disappear. Perhaps the bears even feel a bit drowsy.

In any case, the bears are fat. The leaves are tumbling down like a swirling brown snowstorm. The forest underbrush is gone, leaving it open and parklike. Biting insects are but a memory. Roly-poly and growing tired, black bears head off in search of one last need, a winter den.

Obesity is not an undesirable condition among black bears.

OVERLEAF: As winter nears, the bear's metabolism switches from insatiable hunger to undeniable slumber.

CHAPTER FIVE

Winter Miracle

Winter is a time of black bear miracles.

EARLY WINTER WOODS ARE SOMBER WOODS. Leafless trees throw scraggly shadows on a brown forest floor. Small bogland pools are frozen, rimmed in white, while beaver dams begin to ice over. Lakes are darkly cold, nearing the point where they, too, will miraculously sheet over on some windless night beneath blazing Orion. White-tailed deer have moved to thick conifer cover, and the bucks, exhausted from their amorous rutting pursuits, are quiet now, their travels ended, feeding again to replace the fat they have burned during their intensive mating rituals.

Black bears may consume extra water just before entering their den for the winter.

Black bears have slowed down, too. If the fall has been lush, the berries and nuts plentiful, the bears are fat, and wallow as they walk. By the end of October in their more northerly range, some black bears will already have denned. For others, the winter's slumber is but a few days or weeks away. Snow gently falls in large white flakes, or is driven like pellets on the stiff winds of the first real winter storm. All animals are preparing, each in its species' own way, for the long, dark winter months ahead.

I have followed bear tracks well into the middle of November through the Minnesota woods, even though most bears would have denned up by then. Invariably these tracks take me to where a hunter has slain and field-dressed a deer, for this is the month for deer season in my home state. I've often wondered if some bears remain above ground and awake only to take part in this last, predictable feast. It would not surprise me that the adaptable black bear has learned to capitalize on this food source. Once, I even followed the tracks of a black bear that was in turn following the tracks of a wounded doe. The bear must have jumped the doe a number of times during the night, and when I caught up with the bear, he had already caught up with the doe. So much for the theory that black bears only hunt fawn whitetails.

By November, in my part of the world, the tundra swans are hooting along far above, the last of the waterfowl to migrate. Bald eagles are migrating then, too, and the summer songbirds have long departed, with winter birds arriving daily from farther north. It is hard to believe that northern Minnesota is the "south" that some creatures choose as their winter retreat.

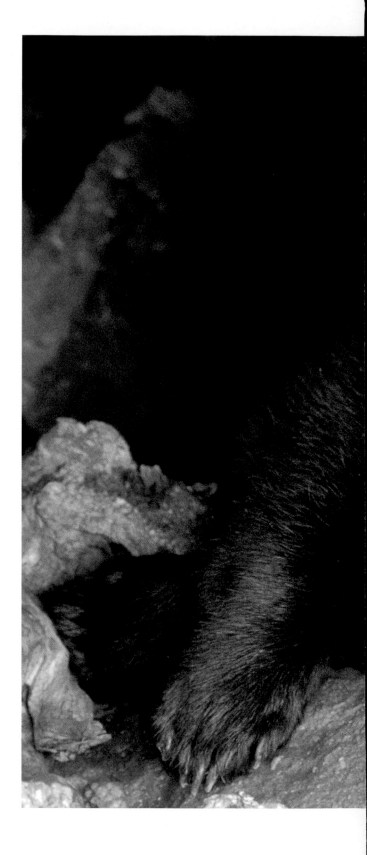

By late October or early November, most black bears have begun hibernation.

Those animals that can migrate are doing so or have already gone. Those that remain must find some way of marshaling their energy and surviving what can be a long, frigid winter. White-tailed deer, their metabolism reacting to the shortening of days, slow their movements, seek dense cover, and reduce their food consumption. Nature has given them the ability to exist on little food, especially once their metabolic rate declines. The short days are spent in search of sun and warmth, or huddled beneath a pine or spruce, shielded from the snow. These dark trees also create a warmer microclimate beneath them. Still, they are awake, and must move and eat during the winter, no matter the cold, no matter the snow. Theirs is a winter of waiting.

But as we all know, black bears neither migrate nor remain awake during the winter. Eons of evolution have remarkably adapted them to survive the longest winter—in their farthest northern range, a winter that may be nearly seven months long. Fat is stored in layers over their entire body. Thick, dense coats of fur are fully grown, layered with guard hairs above and woollike underfur below. Yet these advantages alone are not enough for black bears to survive a foodless winter. Were they to remain active, the fat would quickly be burned, and spring would arrive far too late for them to survive.

Although predators by ancestry, black bears cannot hunt in winter as effectively as the other carnivores with which they share the winter woods. Wolves, swift and working in cooperative packs, can haul down deer to survive, a manner of hunting the bear cannot employ. Foxes prey on grouse or mice, foods too tiny or too swift to be of use to bears. With meat uncertain and vegetable matter hidden by snow or shriveled by cold, black bears must utilize another, very impressive, tool to survive. They hibernate.

Hibernation, of course, is not unique to black bears. Unless, that is, you are talking about the manner in which a bear does it. Among the hibernators, the bear's skill is both different and advanced. But even before the bears slip into a winter's nap, they must first find a place to do so, because hibernation is different from denning. Many animals have dens but do not sleep the deep sleep. Where a bear dens depends much on what part of the black bear range the individual bear is from. But den it will; den it must.

DENNING

By early October, in a year of good food, the feeding binge of autumn is largely over. Properly conditioned black bears are positively rotund with fat. Large bears may have added 150 or more pounds in just the last two months, and even smaller bears will have put on some 75 to 100 pounds. No one knows just what tells the bear that he or she has gained enough weight to survive the winter, but when the fat stores are sufficient, some kind of biological trigger is pulled, and the bear's once insatiable appetite diminishes quickly. Then, it begins to seek a place to den for the winter. During this period the bear drinks more water than is usual, perhaps in an effort to cleanse its system or to fully hydrate its body. For not only will the bear not eat for five to seven months, it will not drink, nor will it defecate.

With winter comes a shift in bear metabolism.

Scientists now think that during the period before complete hibernation, the black bear slips into a sort of walking hibernation, a slowing of its metabolism even though it is still awake. Just as we don't know what actually causes the diminished appetite, we also don't know what factors send the bear into hibernation or into a den.

Most certainly, weather has a role,

Although old stories have bears hibernating in caves, it is really a rare occurrence.

although cold temperatures alone, or the presence of snow, are not enough to trigger hibernation. Still, it is rare for northern black bears to seek their den before the temperatures have sunk below freezing. It is possible that they are also reacting to photoperiod. Perhaps the shortening of days and abbreviated periods of sunlight affect the hormone- and chemical-producing glands, resulting in molecular messages to the brain and metabolism.

Whatever the external factors, fat reserves are likely the most important signal. Sufficient fat means it's time to sleep, and the finely tuned metabolism of the black bear knows exactly when enough is enough.

Black bears in Tennessee, for example, seek out old hollow trees. Those that live in the frozen north search for an underground den to take advantage of the earth's radiant heat and the blanket of snow that is sure to follow. In any case, a denning site should be a place that is secluded—for a disrupted winter nap is a wasteful winter nap. Every time a bear awakens, it burns energy that it can ill afford. And a dry place to sleep is necessary for the obvious reasons; wet places siphon off additional body heat and, come spring, may flood.

For some bears, a mere brush pile may do, and still others build above-ground nests. Such exposed sites are more common in the southern part of black bear country, especially in Florida or Georgia, but there have been ample instances of bears (usually large males) sleeping away the winter above ground in places as cold as Minnesota. These ground nests are built-up areas of leaves, pine needles, and grass—to elevate the bear 1 to 3 feet above the cold ground so it will be above any water that may collect during the winter. And while ground nests may even be the preferred den site of black bears in the extreme southern edge of their range, they are nonetheless still an exception if you consider the entire black bear population.

Most bears choose a protective site. Large, old trees are frequently used, and it may surprise many that, not only do black bears crawl into hollowed-out fallen trees or trees with open bases, but they will climb to great heights and sleep in hollows well up the trunk. Tree-cavity den sites may even be preferred in a few areas of the South.

A 1981 study in Tennessee by G. J. Johnson and M. R. Pelton showed that black bears choose tree cavities rather than ground sites whenever possible. Some tree cavities may be over 50 feet above the ground, but obviously it takes a large tree to provide such a site, and large trees are becoming scarcer these days. Even when available, these tree cavities are frequently only large enough to accommodate smaller black bears, bears able to squeeze through a hole perhaps less than 2 feet in diameter and curl up in a cavity barely 3 feet across. Still, you can understand the attraction of such a site. It is high and dry, and nearly completely free from the threat of any kind of predator.

But if you had to put a number to it, it would be a pretty safe bet that across North America, most black bears sleep below the ground. Some of these sites will be naturally occurring ones, such as small caves. In order to retain body heat and save energy, a bear needs a cave just barely large enough to turn around in. Anything larger would just use up energy as the bear pumped out body heat trying to warm the surrounding airspace. Frequently, these so-called natural caves are no more that crevices between big boulders or beneath a tilted slab, and they often have more than one entrance, which strains the definition of "cave." Think of them more as a

The cavity below the roots of wind-felled trees are frequently used as black bear dens.

crawl space. In fact, in parts of Pennsylvania where humans have moved into bear country, black bears have been known to hibernate in the crawl spaces beneath homes or under decks.

Caves aren't the only underground den sites black bears choose. Far more common across their range are dens they themselves dig. Black bears sometimes choose to dig these "excavation" dens beneath a bush or tree, or enlarge the hole created when a tree tips over in a wind, lifting up its root wad. Such sites have the added structural integrity of the roots, which helps to keep the soil from collapsing above the bear during the middle of winter. The roots, and the bush or tree above, may even add a bit more thermal protection.

A great number of excavation sites, though, are just holes in the ground, dug into a mound or hillside. In some parts of their range, black bears may enlarge a woodchuck den or fox burrow. In other places, they may choose to usurp a coyote den. In mountainous regions, black bears may actually choose to go to a higher elevation to build a den, since the snow will be deeper and fluffier there, and snow is a wonderfully efficient insulator. In any case, excavation dens are usually oblong in shape, just big enough for the bear to turn around, and are accessed through a tunnel of 3 to 6 feet in length.

Whatever kind of den a black bear chooses, it is usually located in some out-of-the-way place. As big and strong as a black bear is, hibernation does put them somewhat at risk of predation. Although not a deep sleeper, a hibernating black bear doesn't rouse instantly, and there are animals out in the wild that

Although dens in hollow trees are a favorite site, most black bears
will den below ground in natural cavities, such as this one.

Black bears are not safe from predators. Wolves have been known
to seek out bear dens and kill the occupant.

would like nothing better than a meal of bear meat. Some of those animals are other bears.

There have been a number of verified instances where large male black bears, which frequently den up later than subadults or females, have opened the den of smaller black bears or sows with cubs to kill and eat them. Researchers have noted at least one occasion when a grizzly bear dug out a black bear, and killed and consumed its cubs. But bears aren't the only predator capable of such behavior.

Throughout the black bear's range, wolves once existed. Today, wolves are limited to the northern portion of that range, but in these regions it is not uncommon to find evidence of wolves killing black bears. Working cooperatively, wolves dig the bear from its den or attack it in its above-ground nest. This is risky, even if the bear is small, because it can be ferocious in self-defense. But wolves driven by hunger are also determined, and if it is large enough, the pack can overcome all but the largest of bears. It may be that the wolves are preying upon bears in less-than-vigorous health—or at least are only successful if the bear is not healthy. Wolves typically watch, sniff, and otherwise

An early snow must have brought out the playfulness in this bear.

examine prey for weaknesses. They challenge many more animals than they kill, for in the challenge they can quickly assess the prey's ability to flee or fight. So, too, by testing bears in their den, may they learn whether what awaits them is a warm meal or a hot fight.

Black bears frequently build a nest within their den by dragging in whatever readily available forest litter can be found—leaves, needles, and grass. This pile may be a foot or more deep, and probably serves the bear both as insulation and as a means of keeping above any water that may seep in. Pregnant sows will give birth during the winter, and while a little water may not be detrimental to the mother's health, it could seriously affect the cubs, if not drown them. A nest helps reduce this risk.

Black bears usually tend to den up in their home range. This may mean a migration back to it if they have been foraging far from home, occasionally a distance of up to 30 miles. Young males, which disperse during the fall, are the exception—they probably will end up denning wherever their wanderings have taken them. And bear territories are "elastic" in nature. They're neither rigidly

defined nor always ardently defended, so denning isn't confined to some preconceived location. That said, it is very likely that black bears somehow note suitable denning sites as they wander during the summer and fall, and work their way back to them as their slumber arrives and feeding ends.

Most den sites are used only once by a black bear, especially those they've excavated, since these holes rarely last more than a year. It is interesting to note that some black bears that have been awakened midwinter will wander to another den site rather directly, as if they had an alternative in mind. Perhaps they did.

While a Yukon black bear may den for 7 months, and a Florida black bear sleep only for 2, most bears will spend about 4 or 5 months in hibernation. A few may awaken once in a while for a short "walkabout" but this is far less common in the North than the South. Generally, once they're hibernating, most black bears need considerable rousing to interrupt their slumber.

During the "sleepwalking" that occurs just before denning, biochemical changes trending toward hibernation are already underway within the bear. The flow of blood to extremities decreases, and the metabolic rate slows to make more efficient use of fat. Then, finally, whether driven by sleepiness or cold weather, the bear enters its den, and hibernation begins.

HIBERNATION

Denning occurs in the Deep South as late as January, and in the far North, as early as the first week of October. Males are usually the last to enter their dens, while pregnant females, or those already with cubs, will be the first to go into hibernation. It is rare, except in the case of a sow with cubs, for a black bear to share a den. Cubs will sleep with their mother for their first two winters, and the experience most likely helps them learn about how to select a good den site.

Upon entering the den, the bear curls up in a fetal position, nose to tail, slightly on its side, and with its paws and legs beneath it. This position keeps its thinner-furred undersides up off the cold den floor. And if the bear is to give birth, it keeps her nipples exposed enough so that the cubs can nurse.

The metabolic miracle that occurs next has been the source of mystery for hundreds, if not thousands, of years. Many early cults worshiped the bear partly because of its feat of being able to slip into what appeared to be death, and then, incredibly, return to life. And although we know today that the bear's hibernation isn't as much of a near-death encounter as once thought, that doesn't make it any less miraculous. For what we have learned in just the last few decades has only caused us to marvel more greatly at the bear's ability.

To understand this, you must first examine how other animals hibernate. Ground squirrels, woodchucks, bats, and many other rodents also hibernate, but the process is vastly different. These animals are frequently called "true hibernators," although that term seems to somehow denigrate the bear's ability, which in reality, is probably an improvement. In true hibernators, their metabolism nearly comes to a complete halt. Heart rates

Northern black bears may face a hibernation as long as six or seven months.

and breathing decrease to perhaps less than a dozen rhythms per minute. Their metabolic rate on the whole falls by 90 percent. Blood flow decreases dramatically, and the animal very nearly freezes solid—body temperature, depending upon the species, falls from somewhere just above 100 degrees Fahrenheit to just under 40 degrees.

That sounds pretty efficient until you contemplate that they can't maintain this level of dormancy for more than a few days. Although the timing changes depending upon the species, every true hibernator must awaken once or more per week. During this period it will relieve itself of waste, perhaps eat a little from any food it had stored, drink if it can find water, and move around enough to get the blood flowing to extremities.

Internally, important functions are taking place. Exercising reduces muscle atrophy and stimulates bone cell growth to keep bones from weakening. The immune system gets a jump start. Dangerous toxins, such as urea or ketones, are flushed from the body. And then the animal again drifts off into complete hibernation, the process repeating itself throughout the winter.

Black bears have improved dramatically on this regimen. Although they do not drop into as deep a sleep as does a woodchuck or ground squirrel, their metabolic rate decreases dramatically. But the real improvement is that they need not rouse for months on end, somehow having evolved the ability to derive all nutritional needs from fat, while developing the means to process poisonous wastes, avoid muscle atrophy, and offset weakening of the bones. As if this weren't

miracle enough, they also give birth and nurse their cubs during this period.

Where the woodchuck's body temperature dropped by over half, the black bear's dips only by about 10 percent—from a normal range of around 104 degrees Fahrenheit down to about 93 degrees. Herein lies the key to why the black bear must enter winter in such extreme obesity. To maintain a near-normal body temperature, the bear will have to burn a fairly high number of calories—thousands per day. Doing so causes the bear to lose about 20 percent of its body weight by spring. Still, this rate conserves far more energy than if the bear were up and moving about. An active bear in winter could not possibly find enough food to eat to avoid starvation.

By maintaining this relatively normal body temperature—even though storms may rage outside and the temperature plummets to 20 degrees below zero—the black bear can also give birth and nurse. It is the only animal known to give birth during a period of starvation.

In addition, bears are more easily roused from their slumber than true hibernators, which probably serves some antipredator strategy. Although a bit groggy when aroused in their dens, black bears can and will charge intruders, and defend themselves.

But if you were to stick your head in a bear den, what you'd see would be a big black ball of fur, with no outward sign of life. The real miracle is what is going on unseen. For unlike the true hibernators, which must rouse themselves, the black bear is taking care of all its biological needs while in a

Just before entering hibernation, the black bear's metabolism slows.

deep sleep. Perhaps the most amazing part of this is the manner in which it avoids the problems normally associated with not passing wastes.

All animals pass wastes because the items excreted pose serious dangers to their bodies. It is, normally, a vitally necessary process. Black bears, however, by burning only fat, have managed to skirt the issue

Tracks in the snow may betray the location of a den.

quite nicely. When animals starve, they begin to metabolize protein. When protein is burned for energy, urea is created and collects, and must be removed from the body in the urine. To not do so would cause death. The fat-burning bruin not only reduces the amount of urea in its system by not burning protein, it derives secondary benefits from the fat.

When fat is metabolized, it produces water and carbon dioxide. Thus, the bear derives its fluid needs from its own fat and exhales the carbon dioxide as it breathes. And by not needing to urinate, the bear's water requirements during winter are greatly reduced. Any urine that is produced is reabsorbed through the bladder wall, rather than expelled. And what little urea is created in the metabolic process is broken down into carbon dioxide, ammonia, and water. The ammonia is recycled to build new protein, which may allow the black bear to actually build muscle while it sleeps, to help offset atrophy. This remarkable system, only now just becoming understood, seems to explain why black bears, although greatly reduced in weight come spring, suffer no loss of muscle.

Animals that are inactive for too long also suffer from degeneration of bone. Not only do they risk the danger inherent in having weak, brittle bones, but dangerous levels of calcium accumulate in the blood. Research by Dr. Ralph Nelson of the University of Illinois College of Medicine indicates that bears also have some as yet unexplained way of recycling calcium so that they can maintain bone mass and strength during hibernation.

and feeding a cub at this time of the year would put an enormous strain on the mother. Hibernation solves the mother's own metabolic problems, but if the black bear were a true hibernator, it could not give birth in a near-frozen torpor.

The answer, as we've already seen, is the bear's unique mode of hibernation, which has a metabolic rate near enough to normal to allow for birth to take place during it. This kind of hibernation also allows the black bear mother to transfer nutrients to her cubs via milk, which is more efficient than through the placenta. This in turn reduces the demands on the mother's fat reserves. Incredible. No other mammal gives birth during hibernation.

Thanks to this "delayed implantation" solution, black bears can breed in spring, when not a whole lot is going on, and concentrate on food in the fall, when most large mammals are breeding. Without delayed implantation, cubs would be born in the autumn, with far too short a period of time to grow before winter. After the sow has fattened, and about the time she dens, the embryos attach to the uterine wall and normal gestation begins.

During the coldest months of the year—late January or early February—the sow gives birth. She is alert during this process. The cubs are born nearly hairless, with eyes sealed shut. They are very small—6 to 12 ounces each and only about 9 inches in length—which is much smaller proportionally than the offspring of any other carnivore. Hibernation dictates this small size, since retaining cubs intrauterine would place demands upon the mother that could not be sustained. This sort of "premature" birth relieves her of some demands of pregnancy,

Beneath the still whiteness of winter, mother and newborn cubs thrive in a snug den.

The inquiries into the black bear's amazing recycling system have proven to be of interest not just to bear researchers and students of nature, but to medical doctors as well. Understanding the bear's process of urea recycling holds promise for helping humans deal with kidney disease. And discovering the bear's technique for bone building in winter may help doctors treat patients with osteoporosis.

BIRTH

Sometime in late January or early February, the pregnant black bear gives birth in her den to 2 or 3 cubs. They aren't very big. In fact, none of them weighs even 1 pound.

One might ask why it is that black bears give birth during the winter. It's a good question. And it has to do with their size. And their cold-weather evolutionary route. And it even has something to do with the fact that they no longer are carnivorous much of the time.

Large mammals have long gestation periods and give birth to offspring that require months to years to mature. For a tropical deer, for instance, living in a jungle is not much of a problem. Food is available pretty much year-round. Weather, except for droughts, isn't severe enough to threaten a developing youngster.

But the black bear must contend with several complicating factors. Its large size (which is an advantage in cold climates) means it has a long gestation period. In order to grow large, it must eat lots of food in a short period. In order to survive in winter (now that it isn't much of a predator), it must hibernate (since it can't migrate), because vegetative foods are unavailable. And, most important, its offspring must be born early in the year so that they can grow big enough to survive their first winter.

So, if the bear cub were going to grow large enough to survive a grueling winter, evolution dictated it be born in late winter. But, such an outdoor birth would be fatal,

Cubs are born in late January or early February.

Most sows give birth to two or three cubs, which begin to nurse soon after birth.

and allows her to nurse them externally, which, although still taxing, requires that she burn less fat.

The number of cubs born to a sow depends upon several factors, not the least of which is the mother's age. Older sows produce larger litters, although for all black bears litter size ranges between 1 and 6 cubs, with 2 or 3 being most common. The older sows are more successful for a number of reasons, one of which may be that they could just be more sexually mature. Certainly, they are more experienced in finding food and, therefore, go into winter in bet-

ter condition and are able to sustain more embryos. Also, bears living in good habitat or in years of good food give birth to more cubs than bears living in poor habitat or bears in years of mast failures.

At birth, the mother licks the cubs clean. This is a common behavior in mammals, one that helps to dry and warm the newborn, and helps the mother and offspring imprint upon each other. Mother black bears also consume any afterbirth, which not only keeps the den hygienic, but helps reduce odors that might attract predators. Generally, while a mammal mother licks her new baby, it is thought that

Mother and cubs imprint upon each other while denning.

she imprints on the infant's scent.

There is some evidence, however, that even though the hibernating mother is awake during birthing, her scenting ability isn't fully functional. Dr. Gary Alt of the Pennsylvania Game Commission discovered this while trying to introduce orphaned cubs to a denning female. Although she sniffs the newcomer, a foster mother readily adopts newborn cubs while still in hibernation, but similarly attempted adoptions after the bear is fully awake usually result in the sow attacking and even killing the orphan as soon as she can smell it well enough to determine that it is not one of her own.

The newborn cubs crawl into the warmth of the prone mother's folds, using their unusually long and sharp claws to pull themselves along. The six black bear nipples are located on the chest and groin, separated in distance by the abdomen. This odd arrangement seems designed to take advantage of the mother's curled, fetal position, which puts all six nipples close together in a warm "pocket" for the cubs to nurse. (The sow's muzzle is also in this pocket, warming the area with her breath.) Although they cannot see until they are 6 weeks old, the cubs find their way to the nipples by homing in on the heat radiating from this region.

While the mother continues to slumber, the cubs are awake and are well cared for despite their mother's sluggishness. Warm and well fed, they are nourished by mother's milk that is about 25 percent fat. In contrast, human milk is about 4 percent fat, while the blubber-eating polar bear's milk is about 40 percent fat. The mother produces milk by burning her own stored fat. Occasionally, she awakens and licks her offspring to stimulate them into defecating. She then consumes the feces as a means of keeping the den clean.

While the cubs nurse, they emit a sort of humming noise, one that can be heard even outside of the den. They nurse every 2 or 3 hours, and each session lasts but a brief time, perhaps 10 minutes. Competition can some-

times occur between cubs, and occasionally the runt of the litter gets pushed around by a larger sibling. As is typical in nature, the mother does nothing about such competition. And it serves to begin the process of eliminating the weak while nurturing the strong.

If all goes well, the cubs are fully furred, big eared (the ears seem to be the fastest growing part at this age!), and strong enough to venture outside once spring comes. By emergence, most cubs will be about 3 to 4 months old, and weigh about 8 pounds. Venturing into their new world will not only prove exciting, but dangerous, for at no other time in their lives will they be as vulnerable.

And then the cycle repeats itself. Eating. Mating. More eating. Denning. And midwinter births. A cycle millions of years old.

OVERLEAF: Mother and cubs emerge to enter a reborn world, and repeat their species' ancient cycle.

When cubs emerge from the den, they weigh but 8 pounds.